LIVING THROUGH
THE ARAB-ISRAELI WAR SINCE 1948

Alex Woolf

Heinemann
LIBRARY

Chicago, Illinois

www.capstonepub.com
Visit our website to find out more information about Heinemann-Raintree books.

To order:
☎ Phone 888-454-2279
🖥 Visit www.capstonepub.com
to browse our catalog and order online.

Edited by Andrew Farrow, Laura Knowles, and Megan Cotugno
Designed by Steve Mead
Original illustrations © Capstone Global Library Ltd
Picture research by Ruth Blair
Production by Eirian Griffiths
Originated by Capstone Global Library Ltd
Printed and bound in the USA

15 14 13 12 11
10 9 8 7 6 5 4 3 2 1

Library of Congress Cataloging-in-Publication Data
Woolf, Alex, 1964-
  The Arab-Israeli War since 1948 / Alex Woolf.—Ed. 1.
      p. cm.—(Living through)
  Includes bibliographical references and index.
  ISBN 978-1-4329-5995-1 (hb)—ISBN 978-1-4329-6004-9 (pb) 1. Arab-Israeli conflict—Juvenile literature. I. Title.
  DS119.7.W633 2011
  956.04—dc22   2011015920

Acknowledgments
We would like to thank the following for permission to reproduce photographs: akg/ullstein bild pp. 17, 37; © Corbis p. 10; Corbis pp. 4 (© Bettmann), 9 (© Bettmann), 20 (© Bettmann), 23 (© Bettmann), 31 (© Bettmann), 32 (© Christian Simonpietri/Sygma), 39 (© William Karel/Sygma), 40 (© Dominique Faget/epa), 43 (© David Rubinger), 44 (© Alain Nogues/Sygma), 49 (© Patrick Robert/Sygma), 54 (© ALI ALI/epa), 56 (© Nadav Neuhaus/Sygma), 58 (© Ricki Rosen); Getty Images pp. 7 Zoltan Kluger/GPO, 12 (ATTA HUSSEIN/AFP), 18 (Keystone-France/Gamma-Keystone), 24 (Central Press), 29 (Rolls Press/Popperfoto), 35 (Keystone), 46 (PATRICK BAZ/AFP), 51 (J. DAVID AKE/AFP), 61 (Uriel Sinai), 65 (David Silverman).

Cover photograph of Palestinian boys throwing stones at an Israeli tank during clashes at Beit Lahya town in the northern Gaza Strip reproduced with the permission of Corbis/© MOHAMMED SABER/epa.

Extract on p. 48 is from Ricks, Thomas M. "In Their Own Voices: Palestinian High School Girls and Their Memories of the Intifadas and Nonviolent Resistance to Israeli Occupation, 1987-2004". Nat'l Women's Studies Assn Journal (New title Feminist Formations) 18:3 (2006), 93 Quote. © 2006 NWSA Journal. Reprinted with permission of The Johns Hopkins University Press.

We would like to thank John Allen Williams for his invaluable help in the preparation of this book.

Disclaimer
All the Internet addresses (URLs) given in this book were valid at the time of going to press. However, due to the dynamic nature of the Internet, some addresses may have changed, or sites may have changed or ceased to exist since publication. While the author and publisher regret any inconvenience this may cause readers, no responsibility for any such changes can be accepted by either the author or the publisher.

CONTENTS

Words printed in **bold** are explained in the glossary.

CAUSES OF THE CONFLICT (1897–1947)

The Arab-Israeli war has been waged for more than 60 years, making it one of the longest conflicts in modern history. It has actually been a series of wars, broken by periods of uneasy peace. It has also involved other forms of violent confrontation, such as street battles, rocket strikes, **terrorist attacks**, and assassinations. The way the war has been fought has varied over the years, but it has always been about the same thing: a struggle between two peoples for control of an area of land. It is also a clash involving two faiths: Judaism and Islam.

PALESTINE AND ISRAEL

The land under dispute is a narrow strip on the eastern shore of the Mediterranean Sea. Since 1948 that land has been known as Israel. Before then, it was known, for much of its history, as Palestine. For many hundreds of years, the land of Palestine was mostly inhabited by Arabs, the great majority of whom were Muslim. The population had always contained a small minority of Jews, but in the late 1800s and early 1900s, Jews began arriving in much larger numbers and began settling the land. It was their arrival that triggered the conflict.

These Jewish settlers in Palestine in the 1890s are gathered at the Western Wall, the remains of the Second Temple of Solomon, in Jerusalem.

ANTI-SEMITISM AND ZIONISM

These Jews came mainly from Eastern Europe and Russia. They left their homes because, during the 1880s and 1890s, there was a rise in **anti-Semitism** in these areas, and Jewish communities came under attack. Jews fled to the United States, Great Britain, Canada, Australia, and South Africa. Some Jews, known as **Zionists**, feared they would never be safe from anti-Semitism as long as they remained a minority in the countries where they lived. They believed that the Jewish people would only find security when they had a homeland of their own. That homeland, they decided, should be in Palestine.

WHY PALESTINE?

The Zionists believed that the Jews had a historic claim to this land. In the first millennium BCE, the land had been the site of the Jewish kingdoms of Israel and Judah. Zionists also believed that the land had been promised to them by God in the Bible. The Zionist movement was formally established in 1897 by journalist and writer Theodor Herzl. It grew rapidly. Between 1904 and 1914, around 35,000 Jews moved to Palestine, mainly from Russia and Poland.[1] They established farm communities in Palestine. The Palestinian Arabs were unhappy about the new arrivals and sometimes clashed with the settlers.

Jerusalem

Jerusalem is a holy city for three major religions: Judaism, Christianity, and Islam. Its significance to Judaism and Islam has made it a key factor in the Arab-Israeli conflict. For Jews, Jerusalem is sacred because it was the capital of ancient Israel and the site of the Biblical Solomon's Temple and the Second Temple. For Muslims, the same location in the city, now known as Temple Mount, was the setting for the Prophet Muhammad's ascent to Heaven. Today, Temple Mount contains the remains of the Jewish Second Temple, as well as the al-Aqsa Mosque and a Muslim shrine, the Dome of the Rock. Israel is determined to keep Jerusalem as its capital city. The Palestinians are equally resolved to make the city the capital of a future Palestinian state.

ARAB NATIONALISM AND WORLD WAR I

At the time the Jews began to arrive, Palestine was a province of the **Ottoman Empire**, a Turkish empire that extended across much of the Middle East and North Africa. By the early 20th century, the empire was in decline. Many of its Arab subjects, including those in Palestine, wished to overthrow their Turkish rulers and form their own, separate nation or nations. During World War I (1914–1918), the Ottoman Empire sided with Germany and Austria against the Allies (Britain, France, and Russia). The Allies expected the Ottoman Empire to collapse after the war, and they planned to carve up the empire between them. In 1915 the British government made a secret contact with Arab **nationalist** leaders. The British persuaded them to rise up against the Ottoman Empire. In return, the British promised they would support the establishment of an Arab nation in the Middle East, to include the territory of Palestine. Then, in 1917, Britain issued the Balfour Declaration (see pages 8–9), giving its backing to the creation of a Jewish homeland in Palestine. Britain appeared to be supporting both sides.

THE BRITISH MANDATE

Following the fall of the Ottoman Empire in 1922, Britain received a **mandate** (authority to administer a territory) over Palestine from the League of Nations (an organization of countries formed in 1919 to promote international cooperation). The mandate was intended as a temporary arrangement before the creation of a Jewish state. Arab nationalists felt betrayed, and many of them rioted and attacked Jewish settlements. The Jews responded by forming a self-defense association, the **Haganah**. A more extreme offshoot of Haganah, called **Irgun**, carried out terrorist attacks against Arabs.

HEADING FOR PALESTINE

During the 1930s, Jewish immigration to Palestine grew significantly, especially after the anti-Semitic **Nazi Party** came to power in Germany. Between 1922 and 1937, the proportion of Jews in Palestine grew from just over 11 percent of the population to almost 28 percent.[2] This increase led to a major Arab uprising in 1936, known as the Arab Revolt. One outcome of the uprising was that the British reversed their earlier policy of support for the Zionists, and they began restricting Jewish immigration into Palestine. After the **Holocaust**, Jewish demands for an independent homeland became

⚠ Here, members of the Jewish self-defense association, Haganah, meet in the 1930s, while Palestine was under the British mandate.

much harder to ignore. By 1945 the Jewish population had risen to just under 33 percent of the total population. In 1947 Britain decided to end its mandate. The growing Arab–Jewish violence, as well as terrorist attacks on government buildings by Zionist **militias**, had made the country, in Britain's view, ungovernable. It requested help from the **United Nations (UN)**, the successor organization to the League of Nations.

THE UNITED NATIONS PARTITION

A committee of the UN recommended that Palestine be divided into two states—one Arab, the other Jewish. This **partition** would ensure that each state contained a majority of its own population. In terms of land area, the split would be 55–45 percent in favor of the Jewish state.[3] Jerusalem would become an international city, split between states.

THE BALFOUR DECLARATION

The Balfour Declaration is one of the most significant and controversial documents in modern Middle Eastern history. The declaration appeared in a letter written by the British foreign secretary, Arthur James Balfour, and addressed to Baron Walter Rothschild, a leader of the British Jewish community. It committed the British government to a policy of supporting the creation of a Jewish homeland in Palestine. The letter was sent on November 2, 1917, a date celebrated to this day by Israelis and Jews around the world as Balfour Day, and observed by Arabs as a day of mourning and protest.

The text of the Balfour Declaration read as follows:

*His Majesty's government view with favour the establishment in Palestine of a national home for the Jewish people, and will use their best endeavours to facilitate the achievement of this object, it being clearly understood that nothing shall be done which may **prejudice** the civil and religious rights of existing non-Jewish communities in Palestine, or the rights and political status enjoyed by Jews in any other country.*

HOW DID IT COME ABOUT?

One of the leading figures behind the Balfour Declaration was Chaim Weizmann, a Russian chemist living in Britain, who was also a passionate Zionist. In 1906 he met Balfour and began trying to persuade him of the need for a Jewish national homeland. During World War I, Weizmann's influence increased. This was due to his development of a chemical process to create acetone, a crucial component of cordite, which was an explosive material needed in the arms industry. The British government was grateful to Weizmann, so it viewed his Zionist aspirations with sympathy.

There were other reasons why Britain may have been willing to support the Zionist cause. Many British diplomats were convinced that the Jews wielded a powerful influence in world affairs, especially in the United States and Russia. Therefore, they believed that helping the Jews would be in Britain's interests. A rumor that Germany (with its own ambitions in the Middle East) was about to make a similar offer to the Jews may have hastened the release of the Balfour Declaration.

CONTRADICTORY OFFERS

In 1915 to 1916, the British High Commissioner in Egypt, Sir Henry McMahon, exchanged a series of letters with the **Sharif** of Mecca, Usayn ibn Ali, which appeared to contradict the Balfour Declaration. Over the course of this correspondence, McMahon promised the Arabs control of the Arab lands, with the exception of "portions of Syria," which had been promised to the French. Palestine lies to the south of Syria and was not mentioned in the correspondence. In 1916 the British and French made a secret treaty, known as the Sykes-Picot Agreement. This divided the Arab lands into British- and French-administered areas. Under this agreement, Palestine was to be placed under international control. After the war, these conflicting statements of British policy were hotly disputed by Arab and Jewish leaders, and they added to the climate of hostility and mistrust.

△ Chaim Weizmann (1874–1952) played a key role in persuading the British government to support Zionist aspirations. He went on to become the first president of Israel.

THE FOUNDING OF ISRAEL (1947–1949)

The Arab-Israeli war of 1947–49 is known to Israelis as the War of Independence and to Arabs as the **Nakba** (which means "disaster"). The war had two phases. The first phase (November 1947–May 1948) was a period of civil war between the Jewish and Arab communities of British Mandate Palestine. The second phase (May 1948–January 1949) was a conflict between newly founded Israel and invading armies from neighboring Arab states.

CIVIL WAR

The United Nations partition plan (see page 7) was accepted by the Jewish community in Palestine, but rejected by the Arabs. When the UN passed the partition resolution in November 1947, riots erupted among the Arab communities throughout Palestine, most violently in Haifa and Jerusalem. Arab volunteer fighters attacked Jewish

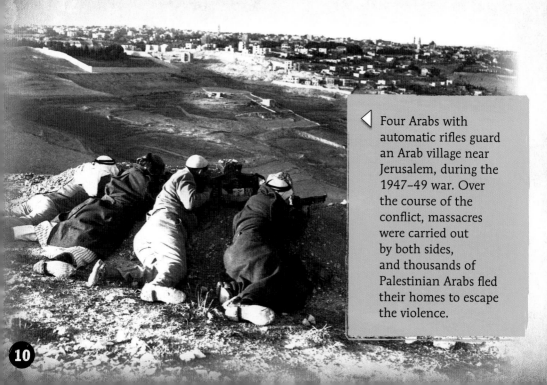

◁ Four Arabs with automatic rifles guard an Arab village near Jerusalem, during the 1947–49 war. Over the course of the conflict, massacres were carried out by both sides, and thousands of Palestinian Arabs fled their homes to escape the violence.

towns and villages across Galilee in northern Israel and laid siege to Jerusalem. In this first stage of the battle, the outnumbered Zionist militias (Haganah, Irgun, and another called **Lehi**) were pushed on to the defensive. The British authorities were unwilling or unable to prevent the violence from spreading—in some cases to civilians.

While Arab **refugees** were streaming out of the country, the Jews were becoming more organized. The leaders of the **Yishuv** (Jewish community) introduced compulsory **conscription** for all Jewish men and women. Funds were raised by supporters in the United States, and the **Soviet Union** supplied them with arms. April 1948 marked a turning point in the battle. Haganah eased the pressure on Jerusalem, while Irgun attacked the city of Jaffa, and the Arabs were driven back in Galilee. Within weeks the Jewish community had captured most of the territory allotted to them under the UN plan.

DECLARATION OF THE STATE OF ISRAEL

Britain's 100,000 troops[1] were gradually withdrawn from Palestine during early 1948, and Britain's mandate came to an end on May 14. On the same day, the Executive Committee of the Yishuv declared the establishment of the state of Israel. The new country was immediately recognized by the United States and the Soviet Union. Over the following days, the armies of six neighboring Arab states invaded Israel. Their intention was to destroy the Jewish state at birth.

The siege of Jerusalem

The 100,000-strong Jewish community[2] in West Jerusalem was isolated from the major center of Jewish population in Palestine, on the Mediterranean coast. The roads to Jerusalem passed through Arab-controlled areas. In December 1947, the Arab military leader Abd al-Qadir al-Husayni laid siege to Jerusalem by attacking Jewish supply convoys to the city. The Arabs also began shelling West Jerusalem. Soon there were food shortages, and a system of rationing was introduced. The Jews responded with Operation Nachshon. In early April, Haganah forces took control of a key road and captured several Arab villages along the route, allowing supply convoys to get through. Over the course of the fighting, al-Husayni was killed. The siege was finally broken in June 1948.

THE DEIR YASSIN MASSACRE

As part of the campaign to lift the siege of Jerusalem, Zionist militias tried to capture Arab villages on the roads leading to the city. One of the villages that came under attack was Deir Yassin, situated on a hill to the west of Jerusalem. The village, which had between 400 and 750 residents (accounts differ[3]), had made a non-aggression pact with the nearby Jewish village of Givat Shaul. Nevertheless, commanders of Irgun and Lehi (also known as the Stern Gang) decided that Deir Yassin posed a threat. Permission to attack the village was reluctantly given by David Shaltiel, the Haganah commander in Jerusalem.

The Deir Yassin massacre sent shock waves through the Palestinian Arab community, and it is remembered to this day. Palestinians commemorate the anniversary of the massacre with a memorial march at the site of the former village.

ذكرى مرور ٥٧ عامًا على مذبحة دير ياسين ٩-٤-١٩٤٨
٢٠٠٥
the memory of 57 years passed on Deir Yassin Massacre

THE ATTACK

In the early morning of April 9, 1948, around 120 fighters from Irgun and Lehi invaded the village from two directions. A truck with a loudspeaker that was supposed to warn the villagers to flee got stuck in a ditch outside the village. The Zionist fighters lacked training and experience. They believed the villagers would flee and were surprised to meet resistance. The villagers assumed they had come to attack the village, but did not realize they intended to conquer it, and so they did not feel the need to flee.

The invaders advanced slowly through the village, attacking each house they came to by throwing hand grenades through the doors and windows and then entering. Sniper fire from the west of the village slowed the offensive. At 10 a.m., a unit of the Palmach (an elite fighting force of the Haganah) arrived with an armored vehicle and a **mortar** and soon silenced the sniper fire.

By 11 a.m., all resistance in the village had ended. Irgun and Lehi fighters then went from house to house, shooting survivors—many of them women and children. Some were taken prisoner and paraded on trucks through West Jerusalem, where they were jeered at, spat at, and stoned, before being handed over to the Arab sector.

LEGACY

The Deir Yassin massacre sent shock waves through the Palestinian Arab community. The atrocity was exaggerated by both sides for propaganda purposes. Arab leaders wished to provoke international outrage and rally their people to fight. Irgun and Lehi wished to frighten Palestinians into fleeing. News of the massacre added to the general sense of panic among Palestinian civilians, and it undoubtedly caused an increase in the flow of Arab refugees leaving Palestine. However, it also strengthened the resolve of neighboring Arab states to attack.[4]

How many died?

Estimates vary on the number of villagers killed. However, a 1988 study by Sharif Kan'ana, who interviewed survivors, concluded that 107 died and 12 were wounded. This is regarded today as the most authoritative figure.[5]

INVASION

In the days following its founding in May 1948, the new state of Israel faced a combined invasion from Egypt, Syria, Jordan, Saudi Arabia, Lebanon, and Iraq. They were joined by the Arab Liberation Army, an army of volunteers from Arab countries, and thousands of other poorly trained volunteers. The stated aim of the invading countries was to destroy Israel and create in its place a "United State of Palestine." They also had ambitions to control parts of Palestine for themselves.

At first, the invaders advanced on all fronts. Lebanon and Syria moved into eastern Galilee. Jordan took the Jewish quarter of Jerusalem's Old City and expelled its inhabitants. Iraq attacked north-central Israel, while the Egyptians took Gaza. Other Egyptian troops advanced toward Jerusalem and cut off the Jewish community in the Negev.

Troop numbers

Country	Approximate troop numbers on May 15, 1948[6]
Israel	29,677
Egypt	7,000
Iraq	10,000
Syria	8,000
Jordan	10,000
Lebanon	2,000
Saudi Arabia	800–1,200
Arab Liberation Army	10,000
Arab volunteers and private armies	52,000

THE TIDE TURNS

Outnumbered by the invaders, Israel appeared to be in a desperate position. But gradually the Israelis' superior training, organization, and experience began to take effect. At the core of the Israeli army was the Haganah, which had existed as a highly effective underground force since 1920. Many other Israeli soldiers had gained valuable experience serving in the British Army in World War II (1939–1945). On May 26, the Haganah, Palmach, and Irgun were incorporated into the newly established Israel Defense Forces (IDF). The ranks of the IDF swelled as more citizens were conscripted, helped by the influx of an average 10,000 Jewish immigrants each month.[7] By the end of the year, the IDF had 108,300 troops.[8] Israel was also assisted by the purchase of arms and military aircraft from Czechoslovakia.

CEASE-FIRES AND TRUCE

The UN managed to arrange a truce, which began on June 11, 1948. When fighting resumed on July 8, Israel captured the key cities of Lod and Ramie, enlarging the corridor between Jerusalem and Tel Aviv. To the north, it captured Nazareth and lower Galilee.

Following a second cease-fire, the final phase of the war began on October 15, 1948. This time, the greatly strengthened IDF encountered success on almost all fronts. The UN arranged a series of cease-fires in late 1948 and 1949. **Armistice** agreements were then signed by Israel and the Arab states, dividing Palestine into three parts. Jordan was left in control of East Jerusalem and the area west of the Jordan River known as the West Bank. Egypt occupied the coastal plain around the city of Gaza, known as the Gaza Strip.

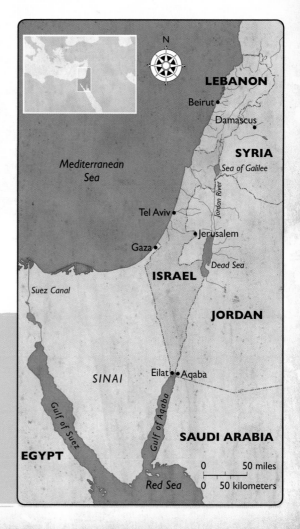

This map shows Israel's borders in 1949, after the war. Israel controlled over 77 percent of the British Mandate Palestine territory—22 percent more than the UN had allotted it.[9]

THE SUEZ CRISIS

The Palestinians were the major losers of the 1947–49 war: the Palestinian state proposed by the UN plan was never established. Furthermore, over the course of the fighting, around 726,000 Palestinians[1] fled their homes to become refugees. Just 159,100 remained in Israel.[2] The refugees moved to the West Bank, the Gaza Strip, and neighboring Arab countries. Israel refused them re-entry after the war. Over the next few years, an uneasy peace reigned between Israel and the Arabs, which ended with a second outbreak of hostilities in 1956.

UNEASY PEACE

The Arab countries refused to sign a permanent peace treaty with Israel or to recognize its borders, which had been established by the armistice agreements of 1949 and known as the **Green Line**. In fact, the Arab states refused to recognize Israel's right to exist at all. The Arab League (an organization of Arab states in the Middle East, formed in 1945) began an economic **boycott** of Israel. The Soviet Union, initially a supporter of Israel, gave its backing to the Arab states as a way of extending its control over the Middle East, and it began supplying them with military aid. Israel continued to receive support, though little aid, from the United States. At this time Israel purchased its arms from France. Another

The Suez Canal

The Suez Canal in Egypt connects the Mediterranean Sea with the Red Sea. It allows water transportation between Europe and Asia without the need to navigate around Africa. The canal was completed in 1869, and in 1882 it fell into British hands when Britain took control of Egypt. The canal's strategic significance soon became clear, especially with the growth of the oil industry in the 20th century. Egypt gained independence in 1922, but in a 1936 treaty Britain retained control of the canal. In 1951 Egypt rejected the treaty, but Britain refused to give up control of the waterway. There followed a tense standoff between the two nations.

Arab-Israeli war looked likely. Yet no one predicted that the spark would be an Anglo-French dispute with Egypt over a canal.

NATIONALIZED CANAL

In July 1956, President Gamal Abdel Nasser of Egypt announced the **nationalization** of the Suez Canal (see box on page 16), placing it under Egyptian government ownership. Britain and France were extremely worried. If he wanted, Nasser could now close the canal to their shipping, endangering their commercial interests in the region. They decided to take back the canal by force. However, they knew that direct military intervention in Egypt risked angering the United States and damaging relations with the other Arab states. So, they negotiated a secret pact with Israel. The plan was that Israel would invade Sinai and seize the canal. Britain and France would intervene as peace brokers, instructing both sides to withdraw to a distance of 10 miles (16 kilometers) from either side of the canal. Britain and France would then argue that Egypt was clearly unable to defend this key route, and it was therefore necessary to place it under Anglo-French control.

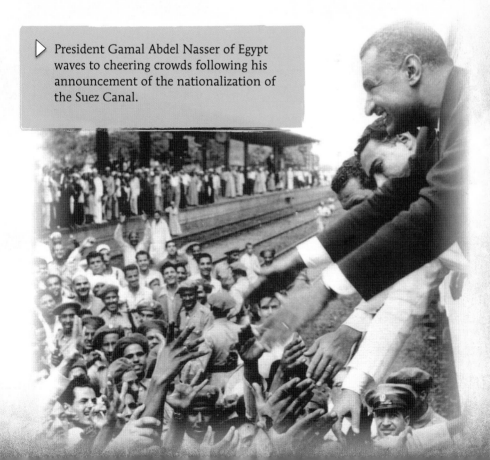

▷ President Gamal Abdel Nasser of Egypt waves to cheering crowds following his announcement of the nationalization of the Suez Canal.

THE PALESTINIAN EXODUS

As a result of the Arab defeat in the 1947–49 war, nearly three-quarters of a million Palestinian Arabs left their homes. The reasons for the mass departure remain the subject of dispute. Supporters of Israel claim the Palestinians left of their own accord, or because they were encouraged to do so by their own leaders. Pro-Arab commentators say they were either forcibly expelled by Zionist soldiers, or they fled in fear of their lives following massacres such as Deir Yassin. When the war ended in 1949, some 25,000 quietly returned to their homes, and Israel allowed a further 10,000 to reunite families.[3] The vast majority, however, became permanent refugees when the Israeli government passed a series of laws forbidding their return and claiming their property. The issue of Palestinian refugees and whether they have a right to return to their former homeland remains controversial to this day.

△ These Palestinian children were made refugees during the Nakba. By the end of 1948, some 450 Palestinian towns and villages had been depopulated, many of which were then demolished.

UNRWA

The refugees fled to neighboring Arab states (see pie chart). For the most part, they were given shelter in refugee camps. A UN organization called the United Nations Relief and Works Agency for Palestine Refugees in the Near East (UNRWA) was set up in December 1949 to provide for their care. UNRWA supplied education, health care, social services, and emergency aid in 59 refugee camps in the West Bank, Gaza Strip, and surrounding Arab countries.[4] The camps began as tent cities and gradually evolved into settlements of small concrete homes.

Where did the refugees go?[5]

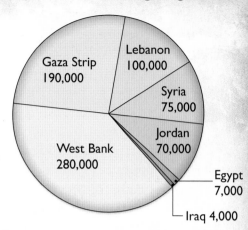

- Gaza Strip 190,000
- Lebanon 100,000
- Syria 75,000
- West Bank 280,000
- Jordan 70,000
- Egypt 7,000
- Iraq 4,000

Refugee experiences

In 2007 Ala Abu Dheer of the Palestine Media Unit[6] compiled eyewitness accounts by those who had fled to Nablus in the West Bank in the 1948 exodus. Their stories offer a compelling account of this period of suffering. During the harsh winter of 1948–49, it snowed heavily, making life very difficult for the refugees living in the tent cities. Tents often collapsed under the weight of snow. The tents were packed closely together—just about 3 feet (1 meter) apart, according to one witness.

Many people suffered from mange or lice, and there were severe shortages of food and drinking water. Some preferred to live in caves rather than tents. One woman said: "In Nablus we lived in caves surrounded by snakes and hyenas; we didn't sleep properly because we were afraid of them." Later, the woman was able to move into a refugee camp built with UN support. She said: "We were given one room to shelter six people. Once my sons were able to earn money we were able to improve our room by adding more rooms and installing electricity and a water supply." Refugees missed the homes and farms they had left behind and frequently expressed their desire to return. One man returned to visit his house in Jaffa after the war. He found a Jewish family living there. He said: "They offered me some coffee—in my own home."[7]

INVASION OF SINAI

Israel agreed to the secret pact with Britain and France (see page 17) for three reasons. First, it wished to reopen the Straits of Tiran (giving it access to the Red Sea), which Egypt had closed to Israeli shipping in 1951. Second, it feared the growing power of its southern neighbor, newly rearmed by the Soviet Union. Third, Israel wished to end the frequent raids carried out by Palestinians and *fedayeen* (militant Arab volunteers) launched from the Egyptian-controlled Gaza Strip. Israel's invasion of the Sinai Peninsula began on October 29, 1956. A battalion of paratroopers was air-dropped into the peninsula near the Mitla Pass, east of the Suez Canal, and sabotaged Egypt's command and control. At the same time, Israeli ground forces advanced on four fronts through the Gaza Strip and Sinai. They were well supported by their air force and encountered little resistance as they converged on the canal. On October 30, Britain and France issued ultimatums to Israel and Egypt to withdraw from the Canal Zone. When Nasser refused, the Europeans began bombing Egyptian forces. Egypt responded by sinking 40 ships in the canal, making it unusable. British and French troops were parachuted in, and the city of Port Said was soon captured.

▽ An Israeli tank maneuvers through rough terrain in the Sinai Desert during the 1956 Suez War.

Gamal Abdel Nasser, 1918–1970

BORN: Alexandria, Egypt

ROLE: Nasser was Egypt's second president, ruling from 1956 until his death. He helped begin an era of modernization and **socialist** reform in Egypt, and he also promoted pan-Arab nationalism (a belief in the unification of the Arab peoples), which included a brief unification of Egypt with Syria (1958–61). He nationalized the Suez Canal and was ultimately successful in his stand against Israel and the old imperial powers of Britain and France during the war that followed. This earned him hero status in the Arab world.

DID YOU KNOW? Nasser's funeral procession through Cairo was attended by at least five million mourners.[8]

WITHDRAWAL

The campaign was proceeding very well, from a military point of view. However, behind the scenes it was causing a political storm. The Soviet Union was threatening to intervene on Egypt's behalf, using "every kind of modern destructive weapon." The United States, fearing an expanded conflict involving the Soviet Union, put severe political and financial pressure on Britain to stop fighting. On November 5 and 6, the British government gave orders for a cease-fire. By December 22, all British and French forces had withdrawn from Egypt. The United States also put pressure on Israel to withdraw from Sinai and the Gaza Strip. Israel agreed to do so, in exchange for guarantees that its shipping would not be blocked in the Straits of Tiran. In addition, Israel was pleased to see a zone established in the eastern and southern Sinai where neither side's forces were allowed, policed by a UN Emergency Force (UNEF). For the two European nations, the campaign was an embarrassing failure, but in Israel, it was viewed more positively. Its armed forces gained confidence from an easy victory, its shipping could pass easily into the Red Sea, and the presence of UN troops brought security to its southern border.

THE SIX-DAY WAR AND THE RISE OF THE PLO

The hostility between Israel and the Arab states intensified during the 1960s. The Palestine Liberation Organization (**PLO**) was established during this period, and its use of **guerrilla** raids and terrorist attacks posed a completely new kind of threat to Israel. The Six-Day War, in June 1967, proved a major turning point, and its legacy has defined the conflict to this day.

THE PLO AND FATAH

The PLO was founded in 1964 at a conference of Arab leaders. They intended the organization to represent the cause of pan-Arab nationalism. The other major Palestinian organization, **Fatah**, led by Yasser Arafat, favored a more purely Palestinian nationalism and distrusted the Arab governments. The Arab leaders hoped to exercise more influence over the Palestinian people through the PLO. However, Fatah was the more **militant** group in the mid-1960s. It began its campaign in January 1965 with an attempt to sabotage Israel's National Water Carrier (NWC). The NWC was a system of pipes, canals, and tunnels that diverted water from the Jordan River to irrigate the drier southern and central parts of Israel.

THE DRIFT TO WAR

The NWC was a source of regional tension because it reduced the flow of water reaching Syria and Jordan. In early 1967, Syria began work on a plan to divert two sources of the Jordan River, reducing the flow of water into Israel and threatening the NWC. The Israeli Defense Forces (IDF) attacked the diversion works. Syria responded by shelling Israeli towns in the north. Both sides launched air strikes against targets across the border, and in April a dogfight occurred between Israeli and Syrian fighter planes. On May 15, Syria received a warning from the Soviet Union that Israel was assembling troops on the Syrian border.

This was untrue, but it worried Syria enough to call on Egypt for help. On May 16, Egypt evicted the UNEF peacekeeping forces from Sinai. Six days later, Nasser closed the Straits of Tiran to Israeli shipping. This was the signal for Arab forces to mobilize. Some 500,000 troops, over 5,000 tanks, and almost 1,000 fighter aircraft assembled on Israel's borders.[1] Israel had already put its army on alert and called up 80,000 reserve troops. The United States warned Israel against a **pre-emptive strike**. Yet Israel feared that waiting for an Arab invasion could place it at a terrible disadvantage. On June 4, the Israeli cabinet voted to go to war.

War of words

Following the closure of the Straits of Tiran, President Nasser of Egypt began issuing increasingly war-like statements. On May 27, he said: "Our basic objective will be the destruction of Israel. The Arab people want to fight."[2] On May 30, Nasser declared: "The armies of Egypt, Jordan, Syria, and Lebanon are poised on the borders of Israel.... This act will astound the world. Today they will know that the Arabs are arranged for battle, the critical hour has arrived."[3]

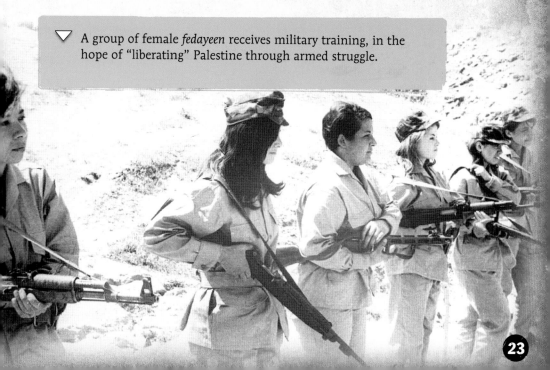

A group of female *fedayeen* receives military training, in the hope of "liberating" Palestine through armed struggle.

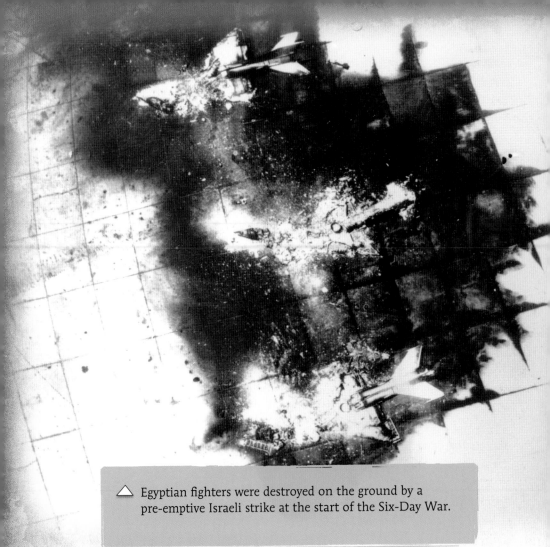

△ Egyptian fighters were destroyed on the ground by a pre-emptive Israeli strike at the start of the Six-Day War.

THE GAZA STRIP AND SINAI

Israel began its offensive at 7:45 a.m. on June 5, 1967, with a surprise attack on the Egyptian air force. Israeli planes attacked in small formations, flying low through previously discovered gaps in the Egyptian **radar network**. Wave after wave of them arrived, subjecting the Egyptian airbases to a sustained, devastating attack. First, they cratered the runways, preventing Egyptian fighters from taking off. They then bombed the aircraft. By the end of the attack, 80 percent of Egypt's bombers and 55 percent of its fighter planes had been destroyed, giving Israel complete command of the Egyptian skies.

While the air attacks were going on, Israeli ground forces began advancing through the Gaza Strip and Sinai Peninsula. After some fierce tank battles, IDF commanders Israel Tal and Rafael Eitan captured Rafah and El Arish in the north. Meanwhile, General Ariel Sharon overcame and defeated a highly fortified position at Abu Agheila by a masterful use of deception, surprise, concentration of firepower, and encirclement. The third Israeli division, under General Yoffe, crossed the sand dunes at Wadi Haridin, which the Egyptians had believed impassable by vehicles, to surprise defenders at Bir Lahfan. Tal's and Yoffe's forces then joined up to capture Jebel Libni. When news of these disasters filtered through to Abdel Amer, the Egyptian minister of defense, he panicked and ordered all units in Sinai to retreat. By June 8, Israel had completed its conquest of Sinai.

THE WEST BANK

On June 5, Nasser sent a message to Jordan's King Hussein. He pretended that Egypt was winning the war against the Israelis and urged him to open a second front against Israel. Hussein gave the order to attack, and Jordanian artillery began shelling West Jerusalem. Israel responded by destroying Jordan's tiny air force and then launching attacks on Jordanian-held territory around Jerusalem. After a day of hard fighting, the Israelis had succeeded in isolating Jerusalem from the rest of the West Bank. The IDF began its assault on the city on the night of June 5. The Jordanians defended it fiercely. One bloody, four-hour battle involved hand-to-hand fighting in trenches and bunkers. The city finally fell on the morning of June 7. Israelis—and Jews throughout the world—celebrated the capture of their sacred city. Other major battles took place in the West Bank towns of Jenin and Nablus. By 8 p.m. on June 7, the entire West Bank was under Israeli control.

Battle statistics

Country	Strength	Losses
Egypt	100,000 troops 1,000 tanks[4] 340 combat aircraft[5]	10,000[6]–15,000[7] killed or missing around 50,000 wounded[8] 338 aircraft[9]
Israel	45,000 troops 650 tanks[10] 196 combat aircraft[11]	275 killed around 800 wounded[12] 19 aircraft

THE GOLAN HEIGHTS

From the start of the conflict, towns and villages in northern Israel had suffered bombing from the Syrian air force and shelling from Syrian artillery on the Golan Heights, a high plateau stretching 40 miles (64 kilometers) along Syria's southwestern frontier with Israel. On June 5, 1967, Israeli jets attacked Syria's air bases, destroying two-thirds of the Syrian air force. Syria responded by intensifying its artillery barrage against northern Israel. By June 8, with its battles on other fronts winding down, Israel began moving its forces north, preparing to capture the Golan Heights. It was a risky operation, since the plateau was full of fortifications up to 9 miles (15 kilometers) deep.

On the morning of June 9, the Israeli Air Force (IAF) began a three-hour bombardment of Syrian positions on the Heights. General David Elazar, in charge of the ground forces, decided to launch five separate attacks. After some hard-fought battles, Israeli forces captured the key positions of Q'ala and Tel Fakhir, giving them control of all the major roads on the plateau. On June 10, the IDF took the town of Masada, and Syrian defenders throughout Golan decided to retreat.

By the end of the Six-Day War, Israel had expanded its territory from about 8,100 to 26,000 square miles (see map on page 15 for previous territory). It would retain these borders until the Yom Kippur War in October 1973.

By nightfall, all resistance had collapsed, and Israel was poised to advance on the Syrian capital, Damascus. Alarmed by this, the Soviet Union threatened to intervene on behalf of its allies, the Arab nations. The U.S. government urged Israel to accept a cease-fire. At 6:30 p.m. on June 10, Israel did so. The Six-Day War was over.

AFTERMATH

As the smoke cleared from the battlefields, it was immediately clear that Israel had won an extraordinary victory. Outnumbered, outgunned, and facing imminent invasion on three fronts, Israel's very existence had been under threat. Yet Israel had not only survived, it had expanded. In just six days, its forces had conquered the Gaza Strip, Sinai, the West Bank, and the Golan Heights, more than tripling the nation's territory. But if the Israeli government believed that the Arab nations would now accept the fact of its existence and that peace would follow, it was mistaken. Within weeks, the Soviet Union was rearming Egypt and Syria.

On July 15, Arab leaders met in Khartoum, the capital city of Sudan, to pronounce the "Three Nos of Khartoum": "No peace with Israel, no negotiations with Israel, no recognition of Israel." To add to its problems, Israel's conquests had brought within its borders 954,898 Palestinian Arabs,[13] most of whom were hostile to their new government. Israel also faced international pressure. On November 22, 1967, the **UN Security Council**, a body of 15 leading countries within the United Nations, adopted **UN Resolution** 242. This called for the withdrawal of Israel's armed forces from territories occupied in the recent conflict. The West Bank, East Jerusalem, the Gaza Strip, Sinai, and the Golan Heights collectively became known as the **Occupied Territories**, and Israel's possession of them would become a major obstacle to peace in the region in the years to come.

Battle statistics

Country	Strength	Losses
Syria	40,000 troops, 260 tanks[14]	2,500 killed, 5,000 wounded, 591 taken prisoner, 59 aircraft[15]
Israel	3 armored brigades, 5 infantry brigades[16]	115 killed, 306 wounded[17]

THE PLO

The resounding defeat of the Arab nations in the Six-Day War destroyed their credibility in the eyes of the Palestinian people. They lost influence in the Palestine Liberation Organization (PLO) (see page 22), which thereafter became a more independent and increasingly militant organization. Fatah joined the PLO in 1967, and the Fatah leader, Yasser Arafat, was appointed chairman of the PLO in 1969. The PLO was, in fact, an umbrella organization for eight Palestinian factions (smaller groups), of which Fatah was the largest. Each faction represented a different strand of opinion within the Palestinian population, but all shared the common goal of destroying Israel and replacing it with a Palestinian state.

BATTLE OF KARAMEH

After 1967 the PLO engaged in guerrilla warfare against Israel. From its bases in the Occupied Territories—Jordan, Lebanon, and Syria— the PLO launched hundreds of raids and artillery attacks on Israeli military and civilian targets. In March 1968, Israel hit back with a military strike on Fatah headquarters in the village of Karameh, Jordan. The Israeli Defense Forces (IDF) were surprised when Fatah stood its ground, supported by the Jordanian Army, and the IDF commanders ordered a tactical retreat. Although Israel achieved its objectives, Fatah considered the Battle of Karameh a great victory because of the IDF's hasty withdrawal. The battle greatly added to the prestige of Fatah and the PLO among Palestinians.

However, relations between the PLO and the Jordanian government were deteriorating. By 1969 the PLO was acting like a separate country within Jordan, with its own alternative political organization and military. Jordan's King Hussein feared that PLO attacks on Israel from Jordanian territory might provoke a full-scale Israeli invasion of his country. After the PFLP (a faction of the PLO) blew up three hijacked airliners at a Jordanian airport on September 1, 1970, the king's patience ran out. He declared **martial law**, and the Jordanian army attacked Palestinian camps throughout Jordan. Thousands died in a 10-day civil war known as Black September. Driven from Jordan, the PLO re-established itself in Lebanon.

TOWARD INTERNATIONAL LEGITIMACY

In 1974 Yasser Arafat addressed the **UN General Assembly**. He said, "Today I have come bearing an olive branch [representing peace] and a freedom fighter's gun. Do not let the olive branch fall from my hand." His speech increased international sympathy for the Palestinian cause. Shortly afterward, the PLO was given "observer status" at the UN, and resolutions were passed recognizing the rights of the Palestinians to form their own government, instead of living under Israeli occupation.

Terror attacks

During the early 1970s, PLO factions carried out a number of high-profile terrorist attacks against Israel and Israeli targets around the world. These included bombings, aircraft hijackings, hostage-takings, and assassinations. The most notorious incident occurred in September 1972, when 11 Israeli athletes competing at the Olympic Games in Munich, West Germany, were taken hostage and later killed by their captors during a rescue attempt. By 1975 the PLO leadership began pursuing a different strategy. It decided to end its terror campaign and try to gain acceptance by the international community as the legitimate voice of the Palestinian people.

▽ On September 12, 1970, three airliners, hijacked by Palestinian terrorists, were blown up at Dawson's Field, Jordan.

THE YOM KIPPUR WAR (1967–1979)

The 12 years that followed the Six-Day War witnessed dramatic shifts in the relationship between Egypt and Israel. Between 1967 and 1970, they remained enemies. When peace overtures from Egypt in the early 1970s fell on deaf Israeli ears, the stage was set for another war in 1973. However, out of the ashes of that conflict emerged an opportunity for real peace between the two nations.

WAR OF ATTRITION

In 1967 the cease-fire between Egypt and Israel was broken when Egypt launched the so-called "War of **Attrition**." It took the form of artillery bombardments, air strikes, and commando raids into the Israeli-held Sinai. Israel responded with some ferocious counter-offensives. Egypt had hoped to force Israel into withdrawing from Sinai. However, by 1970 it was clear that the new, hard-line Israeli government led by Golda Meir was in no mood to give in. A second cease-fire was negotiated in August 1970. Shortly afterward, President Nasser of Egypt died. His successor, Anwar Sadat, was more willing to negotiate, though just as determined to win back the lost territory. He offered to make peace if Israel would agree to withdraw from Sinai, but Israel refused. So, Sadat began making plans for war.

Sadat obtained Syrian support for military action and began building up his armed forces. In early October, the Israeli government ignored **intelligence** warnings of an imminent attack. It thought that Egypt was not ready to fight. But at 2 p.m. on the afternoon of October 6, 1973, Egypt and Syria launched a joint invasion of Israel. They chose Yom Kippur, the holiest day in the Jewish calendar, when people fasted and prayed and day-to-day business in Israel came to a virtual standstill. The attack took Israel completely by surprise.

EGYPT INVADES

Under cover of artillery, 32,000 Egyptian infantry crossed the Suez Canal. They were armed with anti-tank weapons and rocket-propelled grenades, which overwhelmed the shocked Israeli defenses and prevented a counter-attack. The Egyptian advance was also shielded by surface-to-air missiles (SAMs), which disrupted Israeli air support. This enabled the attackers to set up **beachheads** on the eastern bank of the canal. By the evening of October 7, Egypt had 100,000 men and over 1,000 tanks in Sinai.[1] After consolidating their gains, the Egyptians launched a second offensive on October 14. Their forces advanced in six separate columns along a 99-mile (160-kilometer) front. However, they had now moved beyond the range of their SAM shield and were overwhelmed by better-armed Israeli forces. The Egyptians lost over 250 tanks and hundreds of troops. This proved to be the turning point of the war.[2]

BIOGRAPHY

Golda Meir, 1898–1978

BORN: Kiev, Russia

ROLE: Known as the "Iron Lady" of Israeli politics, Golda Meir was Israel's fourth prime minister, serving from 1969 to 1974. She arrived in Palestine in her twenties and became active in the Histadrut trade union movement. In 1949 she was appointed Israel's first ambassador to the Soviet Union. She also won a seat in the Knesset (Israeli parliament), serving as minister of labor and foreign minister before becoming prime minister. She was known for her strong will and nationalism. She once said: "There are no Palestinians."

COUNTER-ATTACK

A planned counter-attack by General Sharon, to sneak behind Egyptian lines and cross the canal, was approved on October 16. After some fierce fighting, the Israeli Defense Forces (IDF) managed to establish a **bridgehead**. The Egyptian Third Army was almost completely surrounded and cut off. The UN imposed a cease-fire on October 22. However, both sides ignored it. Israel tried to complete its encirclement of the Third Army, and the Egyptians fought back. A second UN cease-fire came into effect on October 25, ending the war.

THE GOLAN HEIGHTS

The Syrian offensive started at the same time as the Egyptian attacks. Air strikes and a huge artillery barrage were immediately followed by advancing tanks and infantry. In the northern Golan, a fierce battle raged for three days between 500 Syrian and 100 Israeli tanks. On October 9, the remaining 20 Israeli tanks counter-attacked against a much larger Syrian force. The Syrians, unaware that the Israelis were almost out of ammunition, withdrew.[3]

▽ This shows an Israeli artillery position on the Golan Heights during the Yom Kippur War. Israeli forces came close to being driven out of Golan during the conflict.

In the southern Golan, the Syrians advanced rapidly and had seven brigades on the plateau by nightfall. Desperately outnumbered and poorly equipped, the Israelis began to consider total withdrawal from the Golan. Due mainly to a few IDF officers, who fought on against desperate odds, the Israelis clung on until reinforcements arrived on October 8. The Israeli Air Force (IAF) returned in strength from the Egyptian front, and Israel quickly regained air superiority over the Golan, even bombing military targets in Damascus. On the ground, the IDF launched a swift counter-attack, driving the Syrian forces beyond the 1967 armistice lines. By the time of the UN cease-fire, the IDF were within 25 miles (40 kilometers) of Damascus.

AFTERMATH

Despite their ultimate triumph, Israelis were deeply shocked by the Yom Kippur War. Losses had been heavy—2,688 troops killed[4]—and in the first desperate days of the war, Israel had come very close to defeat. The politicians were blamed for not taking Sadat's peace overtures more seriously and for failing to prepare the nation for the possibility of war. The intelligence community was blamed for failing to predict the invasion, and several top generals were accused of poor decision-making in the first hours and days of the conflict. Golda Meir and her cabinet resigned in April 1974.

Zvika Greengold

A 21-year-old Israeli tank commander, Lieutenant Zvika Greengold, was home on leave when the Syrians invaded. He hitchhiked to Nafekh, an IDF command center on the Golan Heights, where he encountered a column of Syrian tanks. He commandeered a tank and engaged the enemy alone, moving constantly in the darkness to make them think there were more defenders. He destroyed or damaged 10 Syrian armored vehicles before they withdrew. For the next 20 hours he continued to fight, alone or with others, despite suffering wounds and burns. He was awarded the Medal of Honor for his exploits.

PEACE MOVES

In November 1977, Sadat renewed his attempts to make peace with Israel by visiting Jerusalem. He was the first Arab leader to set foot in the Jewish state. In his speech to the Knesset (Israeli parliament), he offered Israel permanent peace and recognition of Israel's right to govern itself. This was dependent on Israel withdrawing from the Occupied Territories and agreeing to the establishment of a Palestinian state. Israeli Prime Minister Menachem Begin responded six weeks later with a visit to the Egyptian city of Ismailia. He said Israel was prepared to negotiate. However, another nine months went by before a framework for those negotiations could be agreed upon.

Oil crisis

Arab leaders responded angrily to a fourth defeat by Israel. They were particularly angered by the fact that the United States gave Israel military aid during the war. The Arab members of the Organization of Petroleum Exporting Countries (OPEC) proclaimed an oil **embargo** against the United States and other Western countries. The embargo caused massive oil price rises and fuel shortages in the affected countries. It finally ended in March 1974, by which time the United States had negotiated an Israeli withdrawal from parts of Sinai and the Golan Heights.

CAMP DAVID ACCORDS

In September 1978, U.S. President Jimmy Carter invited Begin and Sadat to the presidential retreat at Camp David, in Maryland. After 12 days of secret and often ill-tempered discussions, two agreements were signed. These became known as the Camp David Accords. The first of these attempted to solve the Palestinian issue. It proposed giving the Palestinians **autonomy** (self-rule) for five years, after which the final status of the Occupied Territories would be decided. The PLO and the other Arab states rejected the proposal, because it did not guarantee full Israeli withdrawal from the Occupied Territories and the establishment of an independent Palestinian state. Another obstacle to the agreement was the ongoing building of Israeli settlements in the Occupied Territories. Many Palestinians viewed this as a land-grab by Israel. The second agreement concerned Egypt-Israel relations. Under its terms, Egypt regained control of Sinai (but not the Gaza Strip). In return, Egypt recognized Israel's right to exist and promised to keep its forces at least 31 miles (50 kilometers) from the Israeli border. This led to the Egypt-Israel Peace Treaty, the first between Israel and an Arab state, signed in March 1979. Israel completed its withdrawal from Sinai in 1982.

△ U.S. President Jimmy Carter (center) forged a friendly relationship with Egyptian President Anwar Sadat (right), but he found it harder to work with Israeli Prime Minister Menachem Begin (left).

REPERCUSSIONS

Sadat became a hero in the West, and he shared the 1978 Nobel Peace Prize with Begin. U.S. foreign aid flowed to both Egypt and Israel. However, several Arab nations were angered by Sadat's initiative, and they boycotted Egypt. Sadat also aroused the antagonism of militants in his own country, and he was assassinated by Islamic extremists in 1981. Another consequence of the peace treaty with Egypt was the removal of Israeli settlers from Sinai. Jewish settlements had been established in Sinai from 1967, as they had been in the other Occupied Territories. In 1982 Israel dismantled 18 settlements in Sinai and evacuated the settlers, sometimes by force.

ISRAELI SETTLEMENTS

In the years that followed the Six-Day War, successive Israeli governments encouraged their citizens to settle in the Occupied Territories. For some Israelis, this was simply a continuation of the tradition begun by earlier generations of Zionists who had settled in Palestine. However, now they were doing so against international law.

THE WEST BANK

The expansion of Israeli settlements has continued to the present day, in spite of international pressure for them to be stopped. Efrat, near the Palestinian town of Bethlehem, is a typical West Bank Israeli settlement. It is built on a hilltop and surrounded by a buffer zone, which Palestinians are not allowed to farm. It is serviced by roads, which Palestinians are forbidden to use. Settlers say this is all for security, as settlements have been attacked by Palestinians in the past. But it has the effect of blocking Palestinian movement and fragmenting the territory that Palestinians hope will one day form part of an independent homeland.

The expanding settler population

	1972	1983	1993	2004	2007	2009
West Bank	1,182	22,800	111,600	234,487	276,462	310,600
Gaza Strip	700	900	4,800	7,826	0	0
Golan Heights	77	6,800	12,600	17,265	18,692	19,248
East Jerusalem	8,649	76,095	152,800	181,587	189,708	192,800
TOTAL	10,608	106,595	281,800	441,165	484,862	522,648

Throughout the West Bank, settlements and roads have been constructed around and between Arab settlements, undermining the potential for a Palestinian state. Since the 1990s, this has complicated peace negotiations. Any two-state solution to the conflict (with an Israeli state existing next to a Palestinian state) would require the abandonment of many Israeli settlements.

△ This is the Israeli settlement of Efrat on the West Bank. Efrat has 8,500 residents living in rows of modern-looking white houses with red roofs. Like many settlements, it is growing, with plans to expand to 30,000.

THE PALESTINIAN PERSPECTIVE

For Palestinians, the settlements have made life very difficult. There are over 600 road blocks and other obstacles restricting their movement on the West Bank. The settlements occupy 60 percent of the land and are scattered all over the territory, making it hard to envisage how they can build their own state there. Raja Shehadeh, a Palestinian lawyer and writer from Ramallah, is saddened by the way the settlements have altered the landscape he has loved since boyhood—the way the hills have been chopped and flattened by them. He sees Israel's presence here no longer as occupation but colonization. "If Israel wants peace," he says, "it cannot be on this land."[5]

About land?

Ari Ehrlich, Matan Dansker, and Yadin Gellman are students at a school in Efrat. They accept that their settlement is illegal under international law, and they would even give up their homes if it meant they could have peace with the Palestinians. But they don't see the problem as being about land anymore. **Hamas** leaders aren't interested in Efrat, they say. Dansker says, "The problem is about me being an Israeli. A Jew. It's not about land, it's about destroying us."

OPERATIONS IN LEBANON (1978–1982)

Palestinian refugees had been living in Lebanon since the Nakba of 1948. Their numbers swelled following Israel's victory in 1967. From 1968 Israel and Lebanon began launching cross-border attacks against each other. These escalated after 1971, with the arrival of the PLO in Lebanon after its expulsion from Jordan. In 1978 and again in 1982, Israel launched full-scale invasions of Lebanon.

OPERATION LITANI

On March 11, 1978, 11 Fatah members crossed from Lebanon into Israel and hijacked a bus. After a chase and shoot-out, 37 Israelis were killed and 76 wounded.[1] Israel decided it was time to drive the PLO out of southern Lebanon. Three days later, Operation Litani went into effect. Israel's invasion force, including 25,000 troops,[2] occupied most of the area south of the Litani River, forcing the PLO to retreat north of the river. Five days later, the UN Security Council passed a resolution calling for the withdrawal of Israeli forces from Lebanon. A UN Interim Force in Lebanon (UNIFIL) was set up to restore peace and security to the area. Israel withdrew from Lebanon in June 1978.

Lebanese Civil War

The presence of the Palestinians in Lebanon inflamed already-existing tensions between Muslims and Christians there. In 1975 civil war broke out. The war was fought between the Lebanese Front (LF), dominated by Maronite Christians, and the Lebanese National Movement (LNM), composed mainly of Muslims (including the Palestinians) and **Druze**. By 1976 the LNM were winning. The LF invited neighboring Syria to intervene on its behalf. Syria, with ambitions to extend its influence in Lebanon, did so. It subdued the LNM and brought temporary peace to Lebanon.

TROUBLE WITH SYRIA

Despite Operation Litani and the establishment of a security zone, towns in Galilee, northern Israel, continued to suffer rocket attacks from PLO bases in southern Lebanon. Another concern for Israel was Syria's intervention in Lebanon—Israel and Syria were longtime enemies. By 1982 it was clear that Syria was looking to establish a permanent presence in Lebanon. It had deployed over 30,000 troops there,[3] as well as tanks and anti-aircraft missile batteries. The Israeli government decided that another invasion was necessary, with

△ Here, Israeli forces begin their withdrawal from South Lebanon. The IDF handed over positions along the border to its ally, a Lebanese Christian militia called the South Lebanon Army (SLA). Israel was thereby able to maintain a 12-mile- (20-kilometer-) wide security zone to protect itself from cross-border attacks.

the aim of pushing both the PLO and the Syrians out of Lebanon. Israel's allies in this venture were the **Maronite Christians** of the LF (see box, opposite). By this time, the LF had turned against its former allies, the Syrians, fearing that they had become an army of occupation. Israel hoped to bring about a new, Israel-friendly Maronite Christian government in Lebanon, led by Bashir Gemayel, commander of the **Phalange**, one of the strongest LF militias.

OPERATION PEACE FOR GALILEE

In London, on June 3, 1982, Palestinian terrorists shot the Israeli ambassador to Britain, leaving him paralyzed. The terrorists were not members of the PLO. Even so, Israel felt that it had good reason to launch an invasion of Lebanon, known as Operation Peace for Galilee. IDF ground forces crossed into Lebanon on June 6 in a three-pronged attack. In the west, two divisions converged on Tyre. After overcoming fierce PLO resistance there, they proceeded north along the coast to Sidon. In the center, a third IDF division captured the PLO-held Beaufort Castle, before heading west to Sidon to link up with the coastal force in a pincer movement. Another bitter battle was fought at Sidon, involving house-to-house fighting. The IDF, with its superior numbers and armor, eventually prevailed. By June 8, the Israeli army was in control of southern Lebanon and had reached the outskirts of Beirut, Lebanon's capital and the headquarters of the PLO.

▽ Smoke rises from West Beirut following Israeli shelling. The IDF would sometimes strike at civilian targets if its intelligence informed it that PLO arms and munitions were hidden there.

Israel versus Syria

As the IDF closed in on Beirut in the west, in the east, two Israeli divisions advanced into Syrian-controlled territory. Their initial aim was to establish a presence on the crucial Beirut–Damascus highway, then to turn east toward Syria. This, they hoped, would cause Syrian forces in the Bekaa Valley to withdraw. The Syrians stopped the Israeli thrust 3 miles (5 kilometers) short of the highway. On June 9, the Israeli Air Force (IAF) launched a surprise attack on the Syrian anti-aircraft missile positions in the Bekaa Valley, destroying 17 out of 19 of them.[4] The Syrian air force counter-attacked, and a massive air battle took place involving around 200 planes. The IAF triumphed, downing as many as 86 Syrian planes and losing only 3 aircraft itself.[5] With total air superiority, the Israelis pounded the Syrian ground forces. But they remained just short of the highway when, on June 11, under U.S. pressure, they agreed to a cease-fire with Syria.

THE SIEGE OF WEST BEIRUT

Israel was prepared to stop fighting Syria, but no amount of pressure from the United States or the UN could deflect it from its mission to destroy the PLO in Lebanon. The IDF surrounded Beirut with tanks and self-propelled guns, trapping some 15,000 PLO fighters in the western part of the city. For 70 days, the Israelis bombarded PLO positions continuously from land, sea, and air. Food, water, and power supplies were cut, and large parts of the city were reduced to rubble. The Beirut newspaper, *An Nahar*, claimed that 5,515 people died in the siege. Of these, around 1,500 were PLO fighters.[6] At first, PLO leader Yasser Arafat was defiant, vowing to fight to the last man. But in late June, the Lebanese government pleaded with him to spare the civilian population from further suffering. This prompted Arafat to inform the U.S. ambassador that he was prepared to withdraw the PLO from West Beirut. It took until August for U.S. mediators to agree to a cease-fire. The evacuation of PLO fighters began on August 21, 1982.

CITY UNDER SIEGE

The siege of West Beirut lasted 70 days, from June 13 to August 21, 1982. During that time of relentless shelling and terrible deprivation, the city's trapped citizens somehow found ways to survive. According to Iraqi scholar Sami al-Banna, who lived through the siege, the people were able to endure the hardship because of a remarkable sense of community and solidarity. Hundreds of ordinary citizens volunteered for civil defense jobs, acting as medical workers, firefighters, and garbage collectors, working day and night to keep the city going.

BOMBING AND SHELLING

West Beirut endured prolonged periods of intense shelling from land and naval artillery, as well as bombing from the air. The bombardments occurred on an almost daily basis. In one assault, lasting 14 hours, an estimated 180,000 shells were fired, combined with 200 bombing raids. Much of the targeting appeared to be random, perhaps to make the PLO feel that nowhere was safe. During one 20-hour shelling on August 4, the shells and bombs hit mosques, movie theaters, hotels, restaurants, newspaper offices, stores, banks, apartments, and government buildings. An estimated 300 people lost their lives that day, most of them Lebanese. Even hospitals were

Eyewitness

Jacobo Timerman, an Argentinian Jew, gives this eyewitness account of the siege:

Today in Beirut Arab children have their legs and arms amputated by candlelight in the basements of hospitals destroyed by bombs, without anesthetics, without sterilization. It is eleven days since proud veteran Israeli troops cut the electricity and water, and food and fuel supplies. We're in August, a hot August. Rats already outnumber children in the city of Beirut, upon which the best pilots in the world, the aviators of the Israeli Air Force, are exercising their marvelous capacity for precision. From their planes they watch how the buildings of Beirut crumble.[7]

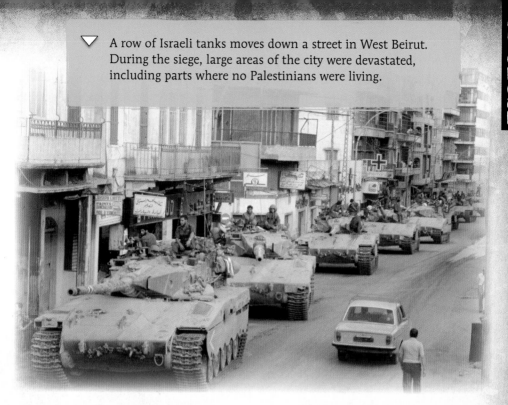

A row of Israeli tanks moves down a street in West Beirut. During the siege, large areas of the city were devastated, including parts where no Palestinians were living.

hit. The Babir Hospital on the edge of West Beirut, near the Israeli gun emplacements, was hit so often that even the badly wounded hesitated to go there. In this frightening atmosphere, many people panicked, abandoning their homes. They moved to different buildings, even different neighborhoods, in a desperate search for security.

CUT OFF

The suffering of the residents of West Beirut was made worse by the Israeli decision to cut off water, electricity, food, fuel, and medical supplies. In peaceful times, water was piped in from East Beirut. With this option closed to them, the residents survived by drilling wells, which soon became unsafe to drink through overuse. Under international pressure, the Israelis occasionally turned the water supply back on, but even then the lack of electricity made it impossible to pump the water through the system. Much of the water gushed wastefully from bomb-damaged water pipes. The lack of water meant that fires caused by bombing often raged out of control. According to aid workers, a number of children died from dehydration during the hot summer, and there were serious cases of dysentery, scabies, eye diseases, and gastroenteritis (stomach flu). The city was overrun with rats, flies, and cockroaches.

AFTERMATH

Israel had succeeded in ousting the PLO from Lebanon, but it had failed to end the threat from Syria, which continued to control the eastern parts of Lebanon. A new Maronite Christian government under Bashir Gemayel was formed in Lebanon, and Israel appeared to have succeeded in two of its war aims, at least. However, Gemayel was assassinated on September 14, 1982, shortly before taking office, possibly by a Syrian agent. Amin Gemayel, brother of the murdered Bashir, formed a Maronite Christian government. But with most of the country under occupation by Israel and Syria, or under the control of militias, the government had little real authority. Nevertheless, in May 1983, Israel signed a peace treaty with Lebanon. Israel agreed to a phased withdrawal of its forces, subject to Syria doing the same. But in March 1984, the Lebanese government, under pressure from Syria and Muslim militias, canceled the treaty.

▽ This young boy and his wounded father are inspecting the bombed-out shell of their apartment in Beirut, following the 1982 Israeli siege.

Sabra and Shatila

Following the assassination of Bashir Gemayel, Israeli Defense Minister Ariel Sharon, backed by Prime Minister Menachem Begin, decided to occupy West Beirut, even though this breached agreements with the United States, Muslim militias, and Syria. Sharon believed that PLO fighters, who may have been responsible for the assassination, were hiding out in the UNRWA refugee camps of Sabra and Shatila in West Beirut. By September 15, the IDF had surrounded the camps. The next evening, Phalangist militia units, eager to avenge their slain leader, entered the camps. They did so with the approval of the Israelis. While Israeli soldiers guarded the camp perimeters and even lit the scene with flares, the Phalangists carried out a massacre. Over the next two days, they killed hundreds of defenseless men, women, and children. The IDF said 700 to 800 died. Other sources claimed up to 3,500 were killed.[9] The attack provoked large-scale protests in Israel and around the world. An investigation, ordered by the Begin government, concluded that Israel bore some indirect responsibility for the massacre. Ariel Sharon was dismissed from his post, but he remained within the cabinet.

PUBLIC PROTESTS

The 1982 invasion of Lebanon was the first war fought by Israel's government that did not enjoy public support in Israel. Unlike previous wars, the Israeli public did not see it as essential to the nation's survival. During the course of the invasion, 368 Israeli soldiers died, and the total death toll of Lebanese, Palestinian, and Syrians amounted to nearly 20,525.[8] For many Israelis, the war was a costly mistake, especially since hostile elements had not been defeated. The Israeli occupation of southern Lebanon stirred up anger among the **Shia** Muslims there, leading to the formation of an Iranian-backed militant group, **Hezbollah**, which would soon present Israel with a new threat to its northern border, even more potent than the PLO. Anti-war demonstrations in Israel demanded withdrawal from Lebanon. In January 1985, the IDF withdrew to the Litani River, leaving a token force to patrol a narrow security zone, with help from the South Lebanon Army. Israeli forces finally departed Lebanon in May 2000.

THE FIRST INTIFADA (1987–1993)

During the 1980s, a growing mood of despair took hold among the Palestinians living in the Occupied Territories. Despite the words and declarations of support from the Arab states, the lives of ordinary Palestinians had not improved. The Palestinians believed that other countries would not take practical steps to help them. The Palestine Liberation Organization (PLO) had been weakened by the Lebanese catastrophe, and its leaders were now in exile in Tunisia. By 1986 around a 1.5 million Palestinians were still living in the UNRWA camps of the West Bank and the Gaza Strip. They faced rising poverty and unemployment, and the expansion of Israeli settlements was making their lives ever more difficult. Under these circumstances, it is perhaps not surprising that a rebellion began.

▽ These young Palestinian boys are fleeing from Israeli soldiers during riots in Gaza City in 1993.

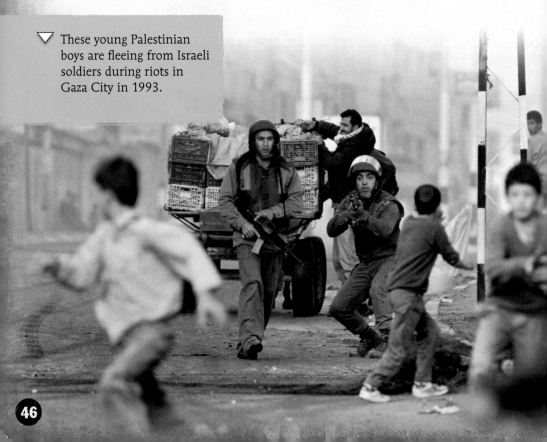

A NEW KIND OF UPRISING

On December 7, 1987, an Israeli truck was driving through the Jebaliya refugee camp in Gaza when it hit two vans carrying Palestinian workers. Four were killed and seven injured. A rumor quickly spread that this was a revenge attack for the stabbing of an Israeli market trader the previous day. By nightfall there were riots in Gaza. These soon spread to the West Bank and East Jerusalem. The uprising came to be known as the **Intifada**, meaning "shaking off" in Arabic. The Intifada began as a spontaneous and leaderless uprising. Soon, local leaders from different PLO factions began to organize it. They formed a new organization, the United National Leadership of the Uprising (UNLU). They employed various forms of resistance, including both violence and civil disobedience. In addition to stone-throwing and fire-bombing, there were demonstrations, strikes, boycotts of Israeli products, and mass refusal to pay taxes.

THE ISRAELI RESPONSE

The Israeli authorities had never experienced a challenge like the Intifada. They responded with brute force. Live ammunition was used against stone-throwers. Crowds were broken up using tear gas and rubber bullets. Houses of suspected ringleaders were bulldozed or blown up, and around 40,000 Palestinians were detained.[1] Abu Jihad, a chief strategist of the Intifada, was assassinated by Israeli agents. World opinion was outraged by what they called Israeli over-reaction. The Intifada's strikes and boycotts weakened Israel's economy. Many Israelis began to see their country's continuing occupation of the West Bank and Gaza Strip as a drain on resources and an obstacle to peace and security. The Intifada continued until September 1993.

Fatalities during the First Intifada[2]

Palestinians killed by Israeli security forces	Palestinians killed by Israeli civilians	Palestinians (accused of collaborating with Israel) killed by Palestinians[3]	Members of Israeli security forces killed by Palestinians	Israeli civilians killed by Palestinians
1,087	75	c. 1,000	60	100

THE ROLE OF WOMEN

The iconic image of the First Intifada is of a Palestinian boy or young man throwing stones. But young women, too, played their role. Reem Zaghmout, who was 12 when the Intifada erupted, remembers older girls barricading the streets with stones, writing slogans on walls, spying, and doing work for the committees that organized protests and demonstrations.

SCHOOLS

Schools were important centers of protest during the early days of the Intifada, before the Israelis closed them down in April 1988. Girls would demonstrate in the schoolyards, chanting slogans and clapping. Israeli forces would shoot tear gas at the protestors and fire warning shots over their heads. The girls would run into their classrooms to avoid the rubber bullets and, often, live ammunition. Almost all girls carried onions, water bottles, and handkerchiefs in their school bags to relieve the effects of tear gas. The onion reduced the irritation to the eyes and nose.

For most of the duration of the Intifada, UNRWA schools, government schools, and universities were closed by military order. For many girls, this left them with little to do but meet and talk with their friends. Education continued, at least for some, in private mission schools, as well as in secret "popular schools" held in

Lina Al-Khairy of Ramallah, who was 13 when the Intifada broke out, wrote in 2005:

I remember that one of our teachers ... asked us to begin to keep a journal because 'these events that we are experiencing are historic'... I found that writing the journal kept me busy at home during the closures, that it gave me a sense of ownership and even self pride about my family, my friends and countrymen and women. I began to feel that I was not alone in my fears when other girls read their journals in class about the same experiences that I was having.[4]

△ These Palestinian women are carrying signs during a
demonstration in Ramallah in the West Bank during
the First Intifada. Thousands of women became involved
in the First Intifada, many of them with no previous
experience of resistance.

people's houses or in mosques or churches. Diana Wahbe of Ramallah
remembers going to one such school in a former teacher's home. The
students were not all at the same level and had to make do with old
textbooks, but she found it an enjoyable experience.

SMUGGLERS AND SPIES

Young women played an important role in supporting young men on
the "front line" of the Intifada. They would offer food and shelter to
those on the run, visit the wounded in hospitals, and smuggle food,
money, and messages into neighborhoods during closures and
curfews. Their work was frequently dangerous, and many were
injured or killed. Some girls kept diaries about the daily events of
the First Intifada and wrote in these their hopes and fears. These
diaries have offered historians a vivid firsthand account of life during
this turbulent period.

MOVES TOWARD PEACE (1988–2000)

In the late 1980s and early 1990s, even though the Intifada was raging in the Occupied Territories, there were hopeful signs that peace in the Middle East might be achievable. There were several reasons for this. Exile in Tunisia since 1982 had left the PLO isolated and weak. The collapse of the Soviet Union in 1991 deprived the organization of Soviet support. On the Israeli side, the experience of the Lebanese invasion and the Intifada convinced many that military strength alone would never guarantee security. Also, the emergence of **Islamism** showed that the PLO was no longer the major threat facing Israel.

MADRID

By 1988 the PLO leadership in Tunisia was remote from its people, who were fighting the First Intifada and wished only to end the occupation, not to destroy Israel. Arafat decided he had little choice but to embark on peace talks. But the United States had barred the PLO from negotiations until it renounced terror and recognized Israel. In November 1988, Yasser Arafat publicly renounced terrorism and, for the first time, recognized Israel's right to exist. This paved the way for peace talks, which finally began in October 1991 at a conference in Madrid, Spain. The conference aimed to tackle all Middle East disputes. The negotiations dragged on through 1992. The violent backdrop of the Intifada added to the atmosphere of mistrust.

OSLO

At the Madrid conference, both sides appealed to their supporters by apparently adopting inflexible positions on the difficult issues. Away from the cameras, however, compromise was easier. A separate set of secret talks began in Oslo, Norway, in early 1993. This was between PLO representatives and a group of Israeli academics. As the talks progressed, Palestinian and Israeli leaders came on board. In August 1993, a draft agreement, called the Oslo Declaration of Principles, was announced. The Oslo Accords were signed three weeks later at the White House, in Washington, D.C.

As U.S. President Bill Clinton looks on, Israeli Prime Minister Yitzhak Rabin (left) shakes hands with Yasser Arafat at the September 1993 signing ceremony of the Oslo Accords. The ceremony witnessed the first handshake between an Israeli prime minister and a PLO leader.

The First Gulf War, 1990-91

In the midst of the Intifada, Israel faced a new threat, this time from Iraq. On August 2, 1990, Iraq invaded Kuwait. A U.S.-led coalition was formed, threatening military action if Iraq did not withdraw. The coalition included a number of Arab countries. Iraq's leader, Saddam Hussein, cunningly attempted to split the coalition by linking Iraq's action to Israel's occupation of the West Bank and Gaza Strip. He declared he would withdraw from Kuwait if Israel did likewise from the Occupied Territories. Hearing this, the PLO felt obliged to support Iraq.

The Gulf War began on January 16, 1991, as coalition forces unleashed Operation Desert Storm: the removal of Iraqi troops from Kuwait. The following day, Iraq launched Scud missiles at Israel. Saddam's plan was to lure Israel into the conflict, knowing that Arab countries would find it hard to fight alongside Israel against another Arab state. Many Palestinians cheered Saddam as an Arab leader prepared to attack Israel. The United States urged Israel not to respond. Israel suffered further Scud strikes, but did not hit back, winning international sympathy for its restraint.

IMPLEMENTING OSLO

Under the Oslo Accords, Israel gradually handed over control of parts of the Occupied Territories to the Palestinians. A Palestinian National Authority (PNA) was established to administer the areas under its control. Israeli restrictions on Palestinian movement within the Occupied Territories were relaxed, and prisoners were released. Elections were held for a Palestinian Legislative Council. Fatah won most of the seats, and Yasser Arafat was elected president of the PNA. Oslo brought benefits to Israel in terms of improved relations with other Arab states. Israel signed a peace treaty with Jordan in October 1994. The Arab boycott of Israel was lifted, and Israel was officially recognized by other Arab states, such as Morocco and Tunisia.

OPPOSITION TO OSLO

A large majority of Israelis and Palestinians supported Oslo and believed it to be the best hope for peace and security. However, a minority on both sides had been opposed from the beginning. To Israel's right-wing, the PLO was still made up of terrorists with whom no deals should be made. They opposed the whole concept of land for peace. Prime Minister Rabin was called a traitor. On November 4, 1995, he was shot dead by a Jewish extremist. Palestinian Islamist groups like Hamas and Islamic Jihad condemned any negotiations with

Jenin

Tulkaram

Nablus

Qalqilya

Ramallah

Jericho

Jerusalem

ISRAEL

Bethlehem

Hebron

■ Areas of Palestinian control

■ Areas of Palestinian civilian control and combined Israeli-Palestinian military control

□ Areas of Israeli control

----- Security wall (begun in 2002)

0   10 miles

0   20 kilometers

◁ This map shows the new distribution of territory as agreed in the Oslo Accords. The West Bank was divided into three areas.

"Zionist imperialists" and refused to recognize Israel's right to exist. Unlike the PLO leaders, whose aim was to create a secular (non-religious) Palestinian state, the Islamists desired an Islamic state under Sharia (Islamic religious) law. They began a campaign of **suicide attacks** that killed many Israeli soldiers and civilians. At the same time, Hezbollah in Lebanon began launching rockets at northern Israel. The violence caused many Israelis to lose faith in the peace process. In 1996 a right-wing, anti-Oslo prime minister, Benjamin Netanyahu, was elected.

WYE RIVER MEMORANDUM AND CAMP DAVID II

In 1998 U.S. President Bill Clinton attempted to restart the peace process by inviting Netanyahu and Arafat to a summit at Wye Plantation in Maryland. Under the Wye River Memorandum, Netanyahu agreed to hand the PNA another 13 percent of the West Bank, in return for a Palestinian pledge to crack down on militants.[1] Netanyahu's administration fell the following year, and he was replaced by Ehud Barak. In July 2000 Clinton invited Barak and Arafat for another summit at Camp David. Barak offered to hand the PNA 94 percent of the West Bank, part of Jerusalem, and the entire Gaza Strip.[2] It was more than any Israeli leader had previously offered, but Arafat, fearing the reaction of the Islamists, could not bring himself to agree to it. He insisted on the whole of the West Bank, and the right of refugees to return to Israel. Arafat returned home to a hero's welcome, but he was criticized by many in the West for his inflexible stance.

IS THERE AN AREA OF AGREEMENT?

The Venn diagram below shows areas of continuing disagreement (outside the overlapping areas) and potential agreement (within the overlap).

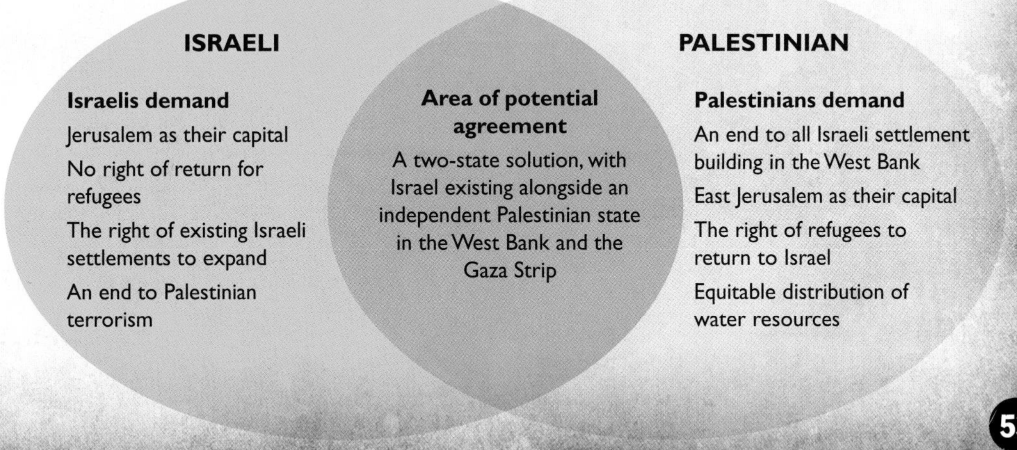

ISRAELI

Israelis demand

Jerusalem as their capital

No right of return for refugees

The right of existing Israeli settlements to expand

An end to Palestinian terrorism

Area of potential agreement

A two-state solution, with Israel existing alongside an independent Palestinian state in the West Bank and the Gaza Strip

PALESTINIAN

Palestinians demand

An end to all Israeli settlement building in the West Bank

East Jerusalem as their capital

The right of refugees to return to Israel

Equitable distribution of water resources

HAMAS

Hamas was founded in 1987 as a Palestinian version of the Egyptian Islamist organization, the Muslim Brotherhood. Hamas's aim was to destroy Israel and establish an Islamic state in Palestine.

VIOLENCE AND SOCIAL WELFARE

From the start, Hamas had two main areas of activity. First, it organized social programs, such as providing schools, hospitals, and religious institutions, and distributing aid to the poor in the Occupied Territories. Second, it carried out military operations against Israel. In 1991 the Hamas leadership set up a military wing called the Izz al-Din **Qassam Brigades**, which engaged in kidnappings and assassinations in Israel. From 1993 Hamas came out against the peace process, and the Qassam Brigades began a campaign of suicide bombings against Israeli military and civilian targets. They enlisted volunteers, including women, and were very effective. In just eight days in early 1996, 59 Israelis died in suicide bombings.[3] The campaign continued until 2005, and it was widely blamed for turning Israeli public opinion against the peace process.

These are members of the Hamas armed wing, the Qassam Brigades. During the Intifada, Hamas fighters waged a guerrilla-style campaign against Israeli soldiers.

POLITICAL POWER

Hamas's high-profile attacks on Israel, together with its provision of social and welfare services, won it a lot of support among ordinary Palestinians. At the same time, the Fatah-dominated PNA was losing credibility due to allegations of corruption and its inability to deliver political gains. Despite the establishment of political institutions, such as the PNA, Palestinians still felt like a people living under occupation. For example, Israel did not hesitate to invade Palestinian towns or close their sea ports and airports in order to disrupt alleged terrorist activity. In the elections for the Palestinian Legislative Council (the law-making assembly of the PNA) in 2006, Hamas won a landslide victory. Despite winning politically, Hamas refused to give up its armed struggle. It stubbornly resisted international pressure to recognize Israel or sign up to the Oslo Accords and subsequent agreements.

But there were some signs of compromise within Hamas. It had lost several of its original leaders to Israeli assassination strikes (see box below), and some of its new leaders were prepared to adopt more moderate positions. For example, they offered a 10-year truce in return for Israeli withdrawal from territories occupied since 1967.

In 2005 Israel withdrew from the Gaza Strip. Hamas fought its bitter rival, Fatah, for control of the strip. Hamas's well-armed and disciplined Qassam Brigades eventually prevailed in June 2007. Fatah was ousted, and the Gaza Strip fell under Hamas's control.

Assassinations

Over the years, many Hamas leaders and senior officials have been killed by Israeli forces, including the following:

Date	Target	Description	Method
1/5/96	Yahya Ayyash	Bombmaker	Bomb in cell phone
7/22/02	Salah Shehade	Leader of Izz al-Din Qassam Brigades	Airstrike
3/22/04	Ahmed Yassin	Co-founder and leader	Helicopter-launched missiles
1/1/09	Nizar Rayan	Top military commander	Airstrike
1/19/10	Mahmoud al-Mabhouh	Military commander	Believed to have been killed by Israeli agents

THE SECOND INTIFADA (2000–2005)

Palestinian hopes had been raised by the Oslo Accords. Many believed that an independent Palestinian state would be established. Foreign aid would flow in, helping them attain a decent standard of living. Yet seven years later, most Palestinians still lived in poor, overcrowded cities or **enclaves**, hemmed in by Israeli settlements and heavily patrolled roads. By 2000 the atmosphere in the Occupied Territories had grown bitter and angry. All it needed was a spark to set off another uprising.

▽ Following Ariel Sharon's visit to the Temple Mount, there were clashes between Palestinians and Israelis.

AL-AQSA VISIT

The spark came on September 28, 2000. Right-wing Israeli politician Ariel Sharon—notorious for his alleged role in the Sabra and Shatila massacre—visited Jerusalem's Temple Mount. This was the site of the Al-Aqsa mosque, a holy Muslim shrine, as well as the Biblical First and Second Temples, which are sacred to Jews. Sharon was surrounded by around 1,000 armed riot police. The controversial visit caused widespread anger. During the protests that followed, Israeli police shot dead six unarmed protestors. Outrage at these killings led to rioting in the West Bank and Gaza Strip.

The First Intifada was fought, for the most part, by stone-throwing youths. In the Second, or Al-Aqsa, Intifada, the Palestinians fought with guns and bombs smuggled into the Gaza Strip from Sinai through secret tunnels. Civilians were targeted as much as security forces, and attacks took place both in the Occupied Territories and Israel. Some 1,500 mortar bombs and 150 Qassam rockets were fired at Israel between September 2000 and June 2003.[1] But the most shocking weapon the Palestinians deployed was the suicide bomber, spreading the violence to the heart of Israel's cities. In 2002 alone there were 46 bombings, killing 237 Israelis.[2]

Israel called upon the Palestinian National Authority (PNA) to crack down on the rocket-launchers and terrorists. Some arrests were made, but the violence continued. Israel began sending its own armed forces into PNA-controlled areas to strike at terrorist bases. In April 2002, in response to a wave of suicide bombings, the Israeli Defense Forces (IDF) reoccupied seven West Bank towns. They shelled suspected terrorist bases, imposed curfews, conducted house-to-house searches, and arrested hundreds of people.

THE END

After a brief cease-fire in June 2003, the uprising carried on through 2004, with more rocket attacks, suicide bombings, and brutal IDF incursions. The Second Intifada finally lost momentum with Yasser Arafat's death in November 2004. It officially ended with a summit in February 2005 at Sharm el-Sheikh, Egypt. Israeli Prime Minister Ariel Sharon and Mahmoud Abbas, Arafat's successor, agreed to a truce, although violence continued sporadically for some time after that.

LIFE DURING THE SUICIDE TERROR

The suicide bombing campaign carried out by Palestinian terrorist groups reached its height during the Second Intifada, when suicide attacks killed more than 500 Israelis. During that period, a sense of danger hung over Israeli cities. Many people were fearful of venturing into public places. Shopping centers, bus stations, restaurants, and entertainment venues, which would normally be thronged with people, were virtually deserted. Israeli novelist David Grossman lived through the Second Intifada. He wrote of people's fear and suspicion of strangers. He described the public reaction when a man in a Jerusalem coffee shop reached into his pocket. "[People] are watching him nervously. Without even realizing they are doing it, people step back, towards the walls. The man draws a box of cigarettes out of his pocket."[3]

▽ Here, Israeli rescue teams assist the injured at the scene of a suicide bus bombing in June 2003. Hamas claimed responsibility for the attack, which killed 16 people and injured over 100.

SURVIVORS

Those who survive suicide bombings must often learn to live with terrible injuries. In August 2002, 23-year-old Israeli soldier Eyal Neifeld was traveling by bus from his parents' home to a military base. A suicide bomber boarded the bus and immediately detonated his bomb, killing nine people. Eyal was blinded and deafened. He suffered a fractured skull, broken eye sockets, damaged spine, and many other wounds. He went through six months of rehabilitation. Cochlear implants enabled him to hear again, but he never recovered his sight.[4] Suicide bombers frequently packed their bombs with nails, spikes, screws, and other metal objects in order to maximize the injuries they inflicted.

The Passover Massacre

The deadliest suicide attack of the Second Intifada was the "Passover Massacre," which took place on March 27, 2002, at the Park Hotel in Netanya, Israel. Thirty Israelis were killed and 140 were injured when a Hamas suicide bomber blew himself up at a Passover Seder (festive religious meal). Most of the victims were elderly, and some were Holocaust survivors. "Suddenly it was hell," said one witness, Nechama Donenhirsch. "There was a smell of smoke and dust in my mouth and a ringing in my ears."[6]

In December 2001, Eran Mizrahi was celebrating his 16th birthday at a Jerusalem restaurant. A suicide bombing sent a nail through his skull, leaving him paralyzed. In another bombing, a young man had 300 individual fragments of metal in his body, several of which penetrated vital organs. He was saved thanks to prolonged surgery. Victims commonly suffered amputated limbs, severe burns, fractures, lacerations, and paralysis. For some, the removal of fragments could do more damage, so they must live their lives with the shrapnel inside them. Many victims suffered psychological damage, such as depression and anxiety. Children seemed particularly affected. Dr. Michael Messing at Hadassah Hospital in Jerusalem recalled hearing statements from young children, such as "Soon I may be killed by a sniper" and "Mommy, please don't go shopping—I love you and I don't want to be an orphan."[5]

THE CONFLICT CONTINUES (2006–2010)

Following the death of Yasser Arafat, there was a brief period of hope that progress might be made on resolving the conflict. His successor, Mahmoud Abbas, was a moderate leader, ready to negotiate with the Israelis. However, by this time the Palestinian people were split between supporters of Hamas and Fatah, and peace was to become harder to achieve than ever.

Since April 2003, a new peace plan had been on the table, proposed by the United States, the European Union, Russia, and the UN. It became known as the Road Map for Peace. The plan had three phases. Phase One required an end to Palestinian violence and a freeze on Israeli settlement expansion. In Phase Two an international conference would agree on temporary borders and matters such as the sharing of water resources. In Phase Three, a second international conference would agree on final borders and clarify the status of Jerusalem, refugees, and settlements. At the Sharm el-Sheikh summit (see page 57), Abbas and Sharon agreed to return to the Road Map. Abbas promised an end to violence, and Sharon agreed to withdraw from occupied Palestinian cities. But the optimism of Sharm el-Sheikh was not to last. Both leaders came under pressure from extremists— Hamas, and the Israeli right-wing. No further progress was made.

OPERATION SUMMER RAINS

In January 2006, Hamas defeated Fatah in the parliamentary elections to win control of the Palestinian National Assembly. Hamas refused to recognize Israel, and Israel, in turn, refused to recognize the new Hamas-led Palestinian government. Hamas's hard-line attitude provoked Western and Arab governments to stop the flow of aid, making life very tough for ordinary Palestinians. Ever since Israel had withdrawn from the Gaza Strip (see pages 62–63), Hamas had been using it as a launchpad for rocket attacks into Israel. To end the attacks and rescue a kidnapped soldier, Israel launched an invasion of the Gaza Strip on June 28, 2006. The invasion was named Operation Summer Rains. The Israeli Defense Forces (IDF) bombarded suspected Hamas bases and destroyed smuggling tunnels. When they withdrew five months later, over 400 Palestinians had died, including many civilians. But the captured soldier was still held, and the rocket fire continued.

△ These Israeli soldiers are preparing for the invasion of Gaza in June 2006.

2006 Lebanon War

While Operation Summer Rains was proceeding in Gaza, trouble flared up once more on Israel's northern border. Israel had suffered relatively few attacks from southern Lebanon since its withdrawal in 2000. But Hezbollah had quietly been building up its forces there. On July 12, Hezbollah launched a raid on Israel. Israel responded with artillery and air attacks on Hezbollah bases in southern Lebanon. The Shia militants hit back with rocket strikes on the cities of Haifa, Tiberias, and Safed. When IDF ground forces invaded, Hezbollah defended fiercely. The war was a propaganda disaster for Israel. Hezbollah bases were often located close to civilian areas, and many Lebanese citizens were killed. Pictures of the deaths and damage inflicted by IDF forces were shown worldwide. The war ended in mid-August 2006. Hezbollah had not been defeated, and so proclaimed it a victory.

DISENGAGEMENT PLAN

Ariel Sharon first voiced his idea that Israel should **unilaterally** withdraw from the Gaza Strip and from four settlements in the northern West Bank in December 2003. He said this would increase the security of Israeli citizens, relieve pressure on the Israeli Defense Forces (IDF), and promote peace between Israelis and Palestinians.

Right-wing Israelis condemned the plan as a betrayal of the settlers. They predicted—correctly—that this action would hand the Gaza Strip to Hamas, who would then use it as a base from which to attack Israel. Many Palestinians, and some left-wing Israelis, suspected Sharon's motives in making this gesture. They saw it as part of a long-term plan to make the remaining West Bank settlements a permanent part of Israel. However, the plan was broadly welcomed by Israel and the international community. It was carried out in August 2005.

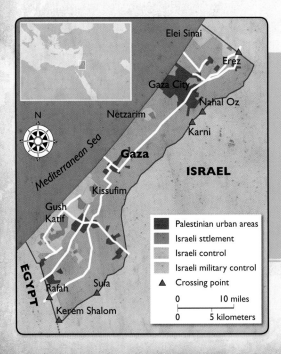

This map shows the Gaza Strip as it was in 2005, prior to the Israeli withdrawal. Following withdrawal, Israel continued to control Gaza's airspace and territorial waters, as well as the movement of goods in or out of the territory.

EXPERIENCES

The evacuation began on the morning of August 15, when security forces entered 6 of the 21 Gaza settlements. Many settlers agreed to leave peacefully, but others had to be dragged kicking and screaming from their homes. Some soldiers were observed crying, and a few even joined settlers in prayer before evicting them. Settlers blocked roads, lit fires, and begged soldiers to refuse orders. A few burned their houses down rather than leave anything for the Palestinians. At Neve Dekalim, 15 Orthodox Jews locked themselves in a synagogue basement and threatened to set themselves on fire.[1] There were violent scenes at Shirat HaYam and Kfar Darom, where settlers barricaded themselves behind barbed wire on the synagogue roof and pelted the security forces with tiles and other objects.

COMPLETION

The last settlers left the Gaza Strip on August 19, and the evacuation of the four West Bank settlements was completed four days later. The last Israeli soldier left the Gaza Strip on September 12, 2005, ending 38 years of Israeli occupation.

"Village of Traitors"

In addition to evacuating the Israeli settlements, the security forces also evacuated Dahaniya, a village of Bedouin Arabs in the Gaza Strip. In 1987, 12 Arab families moved there from Sinai. They had been informers, working for the Israelis against their fellow Arabs. Since then, 15 more Arab families had moved into Dahaniya, all of them informers for Israel during the First Intifada. The Bedouins accepted their new residents, but found their village had become increasingly isolated. Outsiders called it the Village of Traitors. After 1996 the informers were moved to secret locations in Israel, but the village residents continued to be despised as traitors. When the Gaza evacuation was announced, the villagers feared for their security and asked if they could be relocated to Israel, too.[2]

THE BATTLE FOR GAZA

Following the Israeli withdrawal from the Gaza Strip, the territory rapidly descended into political chaos, civil violence, and economic stagnation (inactivity). This was due, in part, to Israel's restrictions on imports into the territory (fearing the supply of weapons to Hamas), as well as weak and corrupt government by the PNA. Relations between Hamas and Fatah became increasingly hostile. Despite being partners in the PNA government, the two organizations had always been bitter rivals. From January 2007 their respective militias began engaging in street battles. In June the conflict erupted into open warfare. At least 118 died in a week-long battle that ended with Hamas taking control of the Gaza Strip.[3] The coalition government was dissolved, and the Palestinians found themselves led by two parties: Fatah in the West Bank and Hamas in the Gaza Strip.

The West Bank barrier

There is probably no better symbol of the entrenched divisions caused by the Arab-Israeli conflict than the 20-foot- (6-meter-) high "security fence" that Israel is currently building around the West Bank. Begun in 2003, its purpose is to protect Israel against suicide attacks, and it has certainly been successful at that. Since it was built, the number of attacks has declined by more than 90 percent.[4] However, opponents of the barrier have said it amounts to an illegal attempt to **annex** Palestinian land. This is because much of it runs to the east of Israeli settlements, placing it beyond the 1949 Green Line. They also say it violates international law according to a 2004 ruling by the International Court of Justice. It restricts the movement of Palestinians and their access to work in Israel.

OPERATION CAST LEAD

A six-month truce between Hamas and Israel expired on December 19, 2008, and Hamas resumed rocket and mortar attacks against Israeli cities. On December 27, Israel launched Operation Cast Lead. This was its second invasion of the Gaza Strip since its withdrawal from the territory in 2005. The war ended on January 18, 2009. It was, once again, both a military victory and a propaganda failure for Israel. Inevitably, many civilians died—759 out of a total Palestinian death toll of 1,390.[5] Israel faced severe international criticism, including accusations of war crimes. Supporters of Israel blamed Hamas for using civilians as "human shields."

EFFORTS TO BRING PEACE

The Arab-Israeli conflict has gone through many phases in its long history. Since the 1970s there have been numerous attempts to find a resolution that satisfies all sides. Yet despite these efforts, by early 2011, peace seemed further away than ever.

As moves toward a political settlement have stalled, hopes have focused increasingly on finding peace through cultural and economic cooperation. One example is the Valley of Peace initiative, a joint project run by the Israeli, Palestinian, and Jordanian governments to promote business and tourism in the West Bank. Another is the Parents Circle–Families Forum, which brings together bereaved families from both sides of the divide. Members give talks on peace and toleration in Israeli and Palestinian schools.

The conflict remains a bitter reality for millions of Palestinians and Israelis, but the efforts of organizations and individuals to spread a message of cooperation and reconciliation give some cause for hope.

△ Veteran Israeli violinist Wafa Yunis gives instruction to Osama Abu Zene, one of five Palestinian youths she is currently teaching. This project is one of several that seek to build bridges between the two communities.

WHAT HAVE WE LEARNED?

The Arab-Israeli conflict has provided many painful and profound lessons, both for its participants and for the world at large. Its long and bloody history has seldom followed predictable paths. At each stage it has thrown up new challenges for people and policy-makers.

The fact that Israel was created as a "Jewish state" demonstrated the central role of religion for early Israelis. And the Jewishness of Israel upset many Arabs who believed that Palestine was an important part of the Muslim world. Some saw the establishment of Israel as a modern equivalent of the medieval Crusaders taking control of the Holy Land. They believed it was a temporary problem that would be corrected in time.

WHAT HAVE THE COMBATANTS LEARNED?

Some Israelis still believe that Israel can hold onto all its conquests and maintain a reasonable level of security, simply by using military force. However, most Israelis have learned that military victories against the Palestinians will not end resistance. Only a political settlement, including the surrender of conquered territory, will achieve that. Many Palestinians have learned to accept the fact that the state of Israel is there to stay, and they are prepared to make a deal with the Israeli government in exchange for peace. But a radical Palestinian minority, and their international backers, such as Iran and Syria, stubbornly refuse to recognize Israel. They are determined to continue their armed struggle until the Jewish state is destroyed.

The Arab states have learned that Israel is a brutally effective military power, especially when backed by the United States, and is difficult to defeat on the battlefield. Some, such as Syria and Iran (not an Arab state, but an important country in the region) have chosen to fight the war by arming militant groups like Hamas and Hezbollah. Others, such as Egypt and Jordan, have chosen to make peace with Israel and suppress the anti-Israel, Islamist opposition within their populations.

WHAT HAS THE WORLD LEARNED?

The world has learned many lessons from the Arab-Israeli war. Over the years, several powerful nations have tried to use the conflict for their own ends. Britain was the first world power to try to meddle in the conflict. During the early part of the 20th century, the British offered support to both sides, thereby making matters much worse. During the Cold War era, the United States and the Soviet Union learned that supporting opposing sides in the Middle East was a dangerous game that, more than once, threatened to escalate the conflict into a wider war. The West, in particular, has learned some costly lessons. For example, support for Israel in the 1973 war led to a damaging oil crisis. And the West's policy of supporting Arab dictators as a force for Middle Eastern stability also looked questionable after presidents Zine al-Abidine Ben Ali of Tunisia and Hosni Mubarak of Egypt fell during popular uprisings in early 2011.

What have YOU learned?

- The Arab-Israeli conflict has roots that go far back in history.
- The Arab states fought in vain to crush Israel in four major wars (1948–49, 1956, 1967, and 1973).
- The Palestinians became a refugee people, whose anger and frustration were given voice by the PLO, Fatah, and Hamas.
- The unity of Arab hostility toward Israel was fractured when Egypt (1978) and Jordan (1994) made peace with the Jewish state.
- The Palestinians rose against Israel in two Intifadas (1987–1993 and 2000–2005).
- The Oslo Accords (1993) and subsequent agreements have led to Israel's withdrawal from certain parts of the Occupied Territories, and the establishment of a Palestinian National Authority (PNA).
- The Palestinians have split between the Islamist group Hamas, which controls the Gaza Strip, and Fatah, which runs the Palestinian areas of the West Bank.
- There is a huge amount of distrust on both sides that will take much effort and probably a long time to overcome.

TIMELINE

1890s	Beginning of modern Zionist movement
1900s	Clashes between Palestinians and Jewish settlers
1917	Balfour Declaration
1922	Start of British Mandate
Nov. 29, 1947	UN General Assembly votes to accept partition plan. War between Palestinian Arabs and Jews begins.
May 1948	British Mandate ends. Zionist leaders declare founding of state of Israel. Neighboring Arab states invade.
1948–49	About 726,000 Palestinian Arabs become refugees
Feb.–July 1949	Armistice agreements signed by Israel and Arab states
July 1956	Nasser nationalizes the Suez Canal
Oct. 29, 1956	Israel invades Gaza Strip and Sinai Peninsula
March 1957	Israel withdraws from Sinai and Gaza
1964	Formation of PLO
June 5–10, 1967	Six-Day War. Israel defeats Egypt, Jordan, and Syria and conquers Gaza Strip, East Jerusalem, West Bank, and Golan Heights.
1967–70	War of Attrition between Egypt and Israel
Nov. 1967	UN Security Council adopts Resolution 242, calling on Israel to withdraw from territories seized in June
1970–71	PLO is driven from Jordan and forced into southern Lebanon
Feb. 1971	Anwar Sadat of Egypt offers peace with Israel, in return for Israeli withdrawal from Sinai
Oct. 6–25, 1973	Yom Kippur War. Egypt and Syria launch surprise invasion of Israel. After initial shock, Israel wins war, but it is a costly victory.
Sept. 1975	Israel withdraws most of its troops from Sinai, and a UN-policed buffer zone is placed between Egyptian and Israeli forces
Nov. 1977	Sadat visits Israel in effort to secure peace
June 1978	Israeli forces withdraw from southern Lebanon
Sept. 1978	Camp David Accords signed by Israel and Egypt at Camp David, Maryland, leading to peace treaty in 1979
June 6, 1982	Operation Peace for Galilee: Israel launches full-scale invasion of Lebanon
June 13–21, 1982	Siege of Beirut begins
Aug. 21, 1982	Siege of Beirut ends. PLO fighters start leaving Lebanon. The PLO goes on to be based in Tunisia.

Sept. 4–16, 1982	Bashir Gemayel assassinated; Sabra and Shatila massacre
Jan. 1985	Israel withdraws from most of Lebanon, maintaining a narrow security zone along border
Dec. 7, 1987	Start of First Intifada
Dec. 1988	Arafat announces the PNC recognizes Israel as a state
Jan. 16, 1991	First Gulf War begins
Jan.–Feb. 1991	Iraq launches 39 Scud missiles at Israel
Feb. 27, 1991	First Gulf War ends. Kuwait is liberated.
Oct. 1991	Middle East peace conference held in Madrid
July 1992	Discussions begin in Oslo between Palestinian and Israeli delegations
April 16, 1993	Hamas carries out its first suicide attack
Sept. 13, 1993	Oslo Accords signed in Washington, D.C. End of First Intifada.
Oct. 1994	Israel signs peace treaty with Jordan. Israeli forces begin phased withdrawal from most of the West Bank.
Nov. 4, 1995	Israeli prime minister Yitzhak Rabin is assassinated
Jan. 1996	Yasser Arafat elected president of the PNA
May 2000	Israeli forces withdraw completely from Lebanon
Sept. 28, 2000	Second Intifada begins when Ariel Sharon visits Temple Mount, sparking widespread protests
Dec. 2001	Israeli tanks surround Arafat's headquarters in Ramallah, keeping him a virtual prisoner
April–June 2002	Israeli forces invade and reoccupy seven West Bank towns, in order to destroy terrorist infrastructure
April 2003	Road Map to Peace, a new internationally backed peace plan, published
July 2003	Israel starts building its "separation fence" between Palestinian-controlled areas and Jewish settlements on the West Bank
Nov. 2004	Yasser Arafat dies
Feb. 2005	Ariel Sharon and Mahmoud Abbas agree a truce, bringing the Second Intifada to an end
Aug.–Sept. 2005	Unilateral Disengagement Plan: Israel withdraws from the Gaza Strip and four West Bank settlements
Jan. 2006	Hamas wins control of the PNA
June–Nov. 2006	Operation Summer Rains: Israel invades Gaza Strip, but fails to end rocket attacks
July–Aug. 2006	Israel invades Lebanon to end Hezbollah attacks. Israel fails to defeat Hezbollah.
March 2007	Hamas and Fatah form a coalition government
June 2007	Battle for Gaza: Conflict between Hamas and Fatah ends in a Hamas victory; Hamas take control of Gaza Strip
Dec. 2008–Jan. 2009	Operation Cast Lead: Israel invades Gaza Strip. Israel inflicts significant damage on Hamas.

GLOSSARY

annex take over a territory and incorporate into a country

anti-Semitism prejudice against Jews

armistice truce in a war to discuss terms for peace

attrition gradual wearing away of an opponent through sustained attack

autonomy political independence and self-government

beachhead part of an enemy shoreline that has been captured and used as a base to launch an attack further inland

boycott cease to deal with something such as a country, as a form of protest against it

bridgehead forward position seized by advancing troops in enemy territory, which serves as a base for further advances

conscription involuntary (forced) enlistment of people for service in the armed forces

curfew official restriction on people's movements, requiring them to stay indoors for specified periods

Druze small Middle Eastern religious sect

embargo official ban on trade with a particular country

enclave portion of territory surrounded by a larger territory whose inhabitants are ethnically or culturally distinct

Fatah Palestinian political and military organization founded in 1958. It has dominated the PLO since the 1960s.

fedayeen Arab guerrillas fighting against Israel

Green Line borders of Israel as agreed to in the 1949 armistice agreements between Israel and its Arab neighbors

guerrilla (adjective) type of warfare waged by small, irregular forces against larger, regular forces

Haganah Jewish paramilitary organization operating between 1920 and 1948, which later formed the core of the Israeli Defense Force (IDF)

Hamas Palestinian Islamist political party

Hezbollah extremist Shia Muslim group based in Lebanon and with close links to Iran

Holocaust systematic extermination of nearly six million Jews by the Nazis during World War II

intelligence	information of military or political value, usually gathered secretly
Intifada	Palestinian uprising against Israeli occupation
Irgun	right-wing Zionist organization founded in 1931, which carried out violent attacks on Arab and British targets between 1937 and 1948
Islamism	belief that Islam is not only a religion, but a political system, and that modern Muslims must return to the roots of their religion and unite politically
Lehi	militant Zionist group operating in British Mandate Palestine (also known as the Stern Gang)
mandate	authority to administer a territory
Maronite Christians	members of a Christian sect of Syrian origin, who live mainly in Lebanon
martial law	military rule, during which ordinary law is suspended
militant	extremely active in support of a cause, often to an extent that causes conflict with other people or institutions
militia	group of people who arm themselves and carry out military operations on behalf of a cause or non-national organization
mortar	type of large gun that fires bombs
Nakba	Palestinian exodus in 1948–49 from the newly created nation of Israel
nationalist	person or group that desires political independence for a country
nationalization	transfer of a business or industry from private to governmental control
Nazi Party	National Socialist Party that came to power in Germany under Adolf Hitler in 1933
Occupied Territories	land conquered by Israel during the 1967 Six-Day War
Ottoman Empire	Turkish empire established in the late 1200s in Asia Minor, eventually extending through the Middle East, ending in 1922
partition	splitting of a country into two or more separate states
Phalange	right-wing Lebanese political party, consisting mainly of Maronite Christians
PLO	stands for the Palestine Liberation Organization, a political and military organization formed in 1964 to fight for an independent state of Palestine

pre-emptive strike attack that is carried out in order to prevent an anticipated attack from the enemy

prejudice (verb) damage or undermine

Qassam Brigades full name: Izz ad-Din al-Qassam Brigades. This is the military wing of Hamas.

radar network number of interconnected installations employing radar—a method of identifying the position of distant objects using radio waves

refugee person who is seeking refuge or a safe place away from war or persecution by going to a foreign country

Sharif Muslim ruler, magistrate, or religious leader

Shia branch of Islam that considers Ali, a relative of the Prophet Muhammad, and his descendents to be Muhammad's true successors

socialist belief that economic production and trade should be owned or regulated by the state

Soviet Union USSR (Union of Soviet Socialist Republics), a communist country formed from the territories of the Russian Empire in 1917, which lasted until 1991

suicide attack attack in which a person deliberately allows him or herself to be killed in the process of killing others

terrorist attack violent attack against civilians and political leaders in order to achieve political aims

unilateral performed by or affecting only one person, group, or country

United Nations (UN) organization of nations, formed in 1945, to promote peace, security, and international cooperation

UN General Assembly main debating body of the United Nations, composed of representatives of all member states

UN resolution decision of the UN reached after a vote of the General Assembly or Security Council

UN Security Council permanent committee of the United Nations, which oversees peacekeeping operations, imposes sanctions, and authorizes military action. It is made up of 15 leading nations, including 5 permanent members: Britain, China, France, Russia, and the United States.

Yishuv Jewish community in Palestine before the formation of the state of Israel in 1948

Zionist member of worldwide movement that sought to establish a Jewish nation in Palestine

NOTES ON SOURCES

Causes of the Conflict (pages 4–9)
1. "The Second Aliyah (1904–1914)," Ministry of Immigrant Absorption, www.moia.gov.il/Moia_en/AboutIsrael/aliya2.htm.
2. "The Population of Palestine Prior to 1948," Table 3, MidEast Web, www.mideastweb.org/palpop.htm.
3. "1947 UN Partition plan—Definition," wordiQ.com, www.wordiq.com/definition/1947_UN_Partition_plan.

The Founding of Israel (pages 10–15)
1. British Forces in Palestine, "Who was there?" www.britishforcesinpalestine.org/whothere.html .
2. "The Population of Palestine Prior to 1948," Table 8, MidEast Web, www.mideastweb.org/palpop.htm.
3. Christina Stewart, "A Massacre of Arabs Masked by a State of National Amnesia," *Independent*, May 10, 2010, www.independent.co.uk/news/world/middle-east/a-massacre-of-arabs-masked-by-a-state-of-national-amnesia-1970018.html; "Deir Yassin Remembered," www.deiryassin.org.
4. Yoav Gelber, *Propaganda as History. What Happened at Deir Yassin?* (Sussex Academic Press, 2006).
5. Yoav Gelber, *Palestine 1948: War, Escape and the Emergence of the Palestinian Refugee Problem* (Sussex Academic Press, 2001), 311.
6. "Israel War of Independence," Zionism and Israel—Encyclopedic Dictionary, www.zionism-israel.com/dic/War_of_Independence.htm.
7. "The Aftermath of the Holocaust—Map: Jewish Immigration to Israel, 1948–1950," Holocaust Encyclopedia, United States Holocaust Memorial Museum, www.ushmm.org/wlc/en/media_nm.php?ModuleId=10005129&MediaId=392.

8. Ahron Bregman, *Israel's Wars: A History Since 1947* (London: Routledge, 2002), 24.
9. MidEast Web, "Israel and Palestine: A Brief History—Part 1," www.mideastweb.org/briefhistory.htm.

The Suez Crisis (pages 16–21)
1. Donald Neff, "1949 Lausanne Conference Seals Fate of Palestine," *Washington Report on Middle East Affairs* (April 1996), 37–38, www.washington-report.org/backissues/0496/9604037.htm.
2. "Population Statistics (Chart V), Israeli–Palestinian Conflict," ProCon.org, israelipalestinian.procon.org/view.resource.php?resourceID=000636.
3. Benny Morris, *The Birth of the Palestinian Refugee Problem Revisited* (Cambridge University Press, 2004), 577.
4. Ron Wilkinson, "Where Are the Tents? It Is a Camp, Isn't It?" BADIL Resource Center for Palestinian Residency and Refugee Rights, www.badil.org/en/al-majdal/item/907-where-are-the-tents?-it-is-a-camp-isn't-it?.
5. Martin Gilbert, *The Routledge Atlas of the Arab-Israeli Conflict*, 7th ed. (London and New York: Routledge, 2002), 47.
6. Ala Abu Dheer, Liam Morgan (ed.), and Alison Morris (ed.), *Nakba Eyewitnesses: Narrations of the Palestinian 1948 Catastrophe* (Palestine Media Unit [Zajel], 2007), 21–104.
7. Ibid, 76.
8. "World: Nasser's Legacy: Hope and Instability," *Time*, Oct. 12, 1970.

The Six-Day War and the Rise of the PLO (pages 22–29)

1. "Precursors to War: Immediate Drift, The Six-Day War," Committee for Accuracy in Middle East Reporting in America, www.sixdaywar.org/content/Immediate-Drift.asp.
2. Isi Leibler, *The Case For Israel* (Australia: The Globe Press, 1972), 60.
3. Ibid.
4. Chaim Herzog, *The Arab-Israeli Wars* (London: Greenhill Books, 1982; updated ed., 2004), 154.
5. Ibid, 152.
6. El Gamasy, *The October War: Memoirs of Field Marshal El-Gamasy of Egypt* (The American University in Cairo Press, 1993), 79.
7. Herzog, 165.
8. A. J. Barker, *Arab-Israeli Wars* (New York: Hippocrene Books, 1981).
9. Kenneth M. Pollack, "Air Power in the Six-Day War," *The Journal of Strategic Studies*, vol. 28, no. 3 (June 2005), 474.
10. Nadav Safran, *Israel: The Embattled Ally* (Belknap Press, 1981), 242–43.
11. "Operation Focus," Middle East Explorer, www.middleeastexplorer.com/Israel/Operation-Focus.
12. "War: Egyptian Front, The Six-Day War," Committee for Accuracy in Middle East Reporting in America, www.sixdaywar.org/content/southernfront.asp.
13. "Demography of Palestine & Israel, the West Bank & Gaza," Jewish Virtual Library, www.jewishvirtuallibrary.org/jsource/History/demograhics.html.
14. www.sixdaywar.org/content/northernfront.asp.
15. Ibid.
16. Herzog, 1982, 186.
17. www.sixdaywar.org/content/northernfront.asp.

The Yom Kippur War (pages 30–37)

1. "Yom Kippur War, Zionism and Israel," Encyclopedic Dictionary, www.zionism-israel.com/dic/YomKippurWar.htm.
2. Ibid.
3. Herzog, 289.

4. Netanel Lorch, "The Arab-Israeli Wars," Israel Ministry of Foreign Affairs, www.mfa.gov.il/MFA/History/Modern+History/Centenary+of+Zionism/The+Arab-Israeli+Wars.htm.
5. Katya Adler, "Challenge of Israeli Settlements," BBC News, March 3, 2009 http://news.bbc.co.uk/1/hi/world/middle_east/7919832.stm.

Operations in Lebanon (pages 38–45)

1. Statement to the press by Prime Minister Begin on the massacre of Israelis on the Haifa–Tel Aviv Road, March 12, 1978, vols. 4–5 (1977–1979), Israel Ministry of Foreign Affairs, www.mfa.gov.il.
2. "Lebanon: Operation Litani, Country Studies Series," Federal Research Division, Library of Congress, www.country-data.com/cgi-bin/query/r-8070.html.
3. "Syrian Troops Leave Lebanese Soil," BBC News, http://news.bbc.co.uk/1/hi/4484325.stm.
4. Matthew M. Hurley, "The Bekaa Valley Air Battle, June 1982: Lessons Mislearned?" *Airpower Journal* (Winter 1989), www.airpower.maxwell.af.mil/airchronicles/apj/apj89/win89/hurley.html.
5. Herzog, 357.
6. Samuel Katz and Lee E. Russell, *Armies in Lebanon 1982-84,* Osprey Men-At-Arms series, no. 165 (1985).
7. Jacobo Timerman (trans. from the Spanish by Miguel Acoca), *The Longest War: Israel in Lebanon* (New York: Alfred A Knopf, 1982), 142–43.
8. Katz and Russell, 1985.
9. "What Happened at the Sabra and Shatila Refugee Camps in 1982?" Palestine Facts, http://208.84.118.121/pf_1967to1991_sabra_shatila.php.

The First Intifada (pages 46–49)

1. "The Intifada, 1987–1992," Salaam, http://salaam.co.uk/themeofthemonth/may02_index.php?l=3.
2. "Fatalities in the First Intifada," B'Tselem, www.btselem.org/english/statistics/first_intifada_tables.asp.

3. "One Year Al-Aqsa Intifada Fact Sheets and Figures: Collaborators," The Palestinian Human Rights Monitor, www.phrmg.org/monitor2001/oct2001-collaborators.htm.
4. Thomas M. Ricks, "In Their Own Voices: Palestinian High School Girls and Their Memories of the Intifadas and Nonviolent Resistance to Israeli Occupation, 1987 to 2004," NWSA Journal, vol. 18, no. 3 (Fall ©2006), 93.

Moves Toward Peace (pages 50–55)
1. "The Wye River Memorandum, October 23, 1998," MidEast Web, www.mideastweb.org/mewye.htm.
2. "The Israeli Camp David II Proposals for Final Settlement, July 2000," MidEast Web, www.mideastweb.org/campdavid2.htm.
3. "Suicide and Other Bombing Attacks in Israel Since the Declaration of Principles (Sept 1993)," Israel Ministry of Foreign Affairs, www.mfa.gov.il/MFA/Terrorism-+Obstacle+to+Peace/Palestinian+terror+since+2000/Suicide+and+Other+Bombing+Attacks+in+Israel+Since.htm.

The Second Intifada (pages 56–59)
1. Herzog, 429.
2. Wm Robert Johnston, "Chronology of Terrorist Attacks in Israel Part VI: 2002," Johnston's Archive, http://www.johnstonsarchive.net/terrorism/terrisrael-6.html.
3. David Grossman, "Israel Is a Clenched Fist, but Also a Hand Whose Fingers Are Spread Wide in Despair," Independent, April 6, 2002, www.independent.ie/unsorted/features/israel-is-a-clenched-fist-but--also-a-hand-whose-fingers-are-spread-wide-in-despair-309246.html.
4. "Eyal Neifeld and Family Visit Florida," One Family Fund, www.onefamilyfund.org/article.asp?ID=2963.
5. Mandi Steele, "Survivors Face Agony in Suicide Attacks," WorldNetDaily, May 30, 2002, www.wnd.com/?pageId=14061.

6. "'Passover massacre' at Israeli Hotel Kills 19," CNN World, http://cnn.com/2002-03-27/world/mideast_1_passover-attack-passover-massacre-attacks-on-israeli-civilians?_s=PM:WORLD.

The Conflict Continues (pages 60–65)
1. Ian MacKinnon, "'Sobbing settlers' Resistance Fades as Troops Clear Homes," The Times, August 18, 2005, www.timesonline.co.uk/tol/news/world/middle_east/article556443.ece.
2. Matthew B. Stannard, "A Quiet Fear in a 'village of traitors,'" San Francisco Chronicle, July 17, 2005, www.sfgate.com/cgi-bin/article.cgi?f=/c/a/2005/07/17/MNG5GDPEJT1.DTL.
3. "Battle of Gaza (2007)," JpostPedia, Jerusalem Post, http://newstopics.jpost.com/topic/Battle_of_Gaza_(2007).
4. Mitchell Bard, "Israel's Security Fence," Jewish Virtual Library, updated July 8, 2010, www.jewishvirtuallibrary.org/jsource/Peace/fence.html.
5. "The Gaza Strip: Operation Cast Lead, Dec 27, '08, to Jan 18, '09," B'Tselem, www.btselem.org/english/gaza_strip/castlead_operation.asp.

BIBLIOGRAPHY

BOOKS

Barker, A. J. *Arab-Israeli Wars*. New York: Hippocrene Books, 1981.

Bregman, Ahron. *Israel's Wars: A History Since 1947*. London: Routledge, 2002.

El Gamasy. *The October War: Memoirs of Field Marshal El-Gamasy of Egypt*. Cairo: The American University in Cairo Press, 1993.

Gawrych, George Walter. *The Albatross of Decisive Victory: War and Policy between Egypt and Israel in the 1967 and 1973 Arab-Israeli Wars*. Oxford: Greenwood Press, 2000.

Gilbert, Martin. *The Routledge Atlas of the Arab-Israeli Conflict*. 7th ed. London: Routledge, 2002.

Herzog, Chaim. *The Arab-Israeli Wars*. Updated ed. Barnsley, South Yorkshire: Greenhill Books, 2004.

Katz, Samuel and Lee E. Russell. *Armies in Lebanon 1982–84* (Osprey Men-At-Arms series, no. 165). Oxford: Osprey Books, 1985.

Morris, Benny. *The Birth of the Palestinian Refugee Problem Revisited*. Cambridge: Cambridge University Press, 2004.

Pollack, Kenneth M. *Arabs at War: Military Effectiveness, 1948–1991*. Lincoln, NE: University of Nebraska Press, 2004.

Safran, Nadav. *Israel: The Embattled Ally*. Cambridge, MA: Belknap Press, 1981.

WEBSITES

www.bbc.co.uk/news/world/middle_east

www.britishforcesinpalestine.org

www.btselem.org

www.fmep.org

http://israelipalestinian.procon.org

www.jewishvirtuallibrary.org

www.lebanonwire.com

www.middleeastexplorer.com

www.mideastweb.org

www.mfa.gov.il/MFA

www.moia.gov.il

www.sixdaywar.org

www.zionism-israel.com

FIND OUT MORE

BOOKS

Abbott, David. *Secret History: Conflict in the Middle East*. North Mankato, Minn.: Arcturus, 2011.

Mason, Paul. *Global Hotspots: Israel and Palestine*. Tarrytown, N.Y.: Marshall Cavendish Benchmark, 2009.

Robson, David. *World History: Israeli-Palestinian Conflict*. Detroit: Lucent, 2010.

Scott-Baumann, Michael. *Access to History: Crisis in the Middle East: Israel and the Arab States 1945–2007*. London: Hodder Education, 2009.

Senker, Cath. *Timelines: The Arab-Israeli Conflict*. North Mankato, Minn.: Arcturus, 2008.

Worth, Richard. *Open for Debate: The Arab-Israeli Conflict*. New York: Marshall Cavendish Benchmark, 2007.

DOCUMENTARIES

Blood and Tears: The Arab-Israeli Conflict (ThinkFilm, 2007)
A documentary about the history of the Arab-Israeli conflict.

WEBSITES

www.btselem.org
B'Tselem is an Israeli human rights organization. The site contains information and statistics about the conflict.

www.fmep.org
Foundation for Middle East Peace (FMEP) is an organization that promotes peace between Israel and the Palestinians. The site contains a wealth of information, maps, and statistics.

http://israelipalestinian.procon.org
This is a non-partisan website that looks at views from both sides of the conflict.

www.mideastweb.org
MidEastWeb is a non-governmental organization in Israel that aims to promote dialogue between Arabs, Jews, and others. The site offers a clear overview of the history of the conflict.

www.mfa.gov.il/MFA
The official website of the Israeli government offers facts about Israel, its history, and the peace process.

OTHER TOPICS TO RESEARCH
The following topics were touched on briefly in this book. If you would like to study them in more detail, here are some websites you can look at. Be aware that some of these websites favor a particular side of the debate!

The history of Zionism
www.mideastweb.org/zionism.htm
www.zionismontheweb.org/zionism_history.htm (pro-Israeli website)

The Nakba
www.alnakba.org (pro-Palestinian website)
www.nakba-archive.org

The Lebanese Civil War
www.globalsecurity.org/military/world/war/lebanon.htm
www.onwar.com/aced/data/lima/lebanon1975.htm

The First Gulf War
www.gwu.edu/~nsarchiv/NSAEBB/NSAEBB39/
www.pbs.org/wgbh/pages/frontline/gulf

The Valley of Peace initiative
www.isracast.com/article.aspx?id=756
www.businessweek.com/globalbiz/content/may2008/
gb20080528_087810.htm

INDEX